AMAZING CHANGE

ORGANIZATIONAL CHANGE LESSONS FROM A
PREACHER'S KID

DONNA STROTHER HIGHFILL

KWE
PUBLISHING, LLC

AMAZING CHANGE

ORGANIZATIONAL CHANGE LESSONS FROM A PREACHER'S KID

Highfill, Donna. *Amazing Change: Organizational Change Lessons from a Preacher's Kid*

Copyright © 2022 by Donna Highfill

Published by KWE Publishing: www.kwepub.com

ISBNs: 978-0-9836496-9-4 (print), 978-0-9836496-8-7 (ebook)

Library of Congress Control Number: 2022908578

Highfill, Donna. Amazing Change: Organizational Change Lessons from a Preacher's Kid

Cover by Michelle Fairbanks - Fresh Design

KWE Publishing—www.kwepub.com

To my parents who allowed me to witness the promise and pain of change in action. To everyone in our church families who were our change evangelists even during the darkest times. And to my siblings who were my fellow change warriors. I love you all.

CONTENTS

FOREWORD

As a creative author, corporate change warrior, and skillful storyteller, Donna Highfill does a fantastic job navigating the widespread problem of how to deal with change, and I definitely know about change.

My name is Robin F. Anderson. I am extremely honored to introduce this wonderful book. As a syndicated writer and author of my own book, *Here... Hold My Wine*, I have been successful working for large companies such as Reynolds Metals Company, JP Morgan Chase, American Express, Truist Bank, MUFG Union Bank, and most recently Texas Capital Bank.

Change is the hardest part of any leader's job regardless of the field you are in. It is an age-old problem. We all have struggled to understand how to manage the impact of change on people in any work environment. And we've struggled, as leaders, to influence people in a constantly changing world.

This author understands the people side of change, and teaches through the use of an analogy from an unexpected place. Sharing her experiences with her father, who was a minister, and their sometimes-hilarious adventures and challenges as a preacher's family, she successfully ties family stories of changing churches to leadership lessons for business leaders.

Organizational culture is a hot topic, and requires extensive people-knowledge. As a young girl, Donna watched the behavior of congregants with the protective ferocity of a daughter, learning lessons about how to read people. Most importantly, she learned how to see the heart and appeal to people from all walks of life which helped her become an effective change leader.

Naturally, Donna became a change consultant for businesses through her experiences. She has brought to my attention so many things I did not know about how to help people handle change and how to lead them forward. Her book is chock full of attention-getting stories and change lessons. At the end of each chapter, the lessons give a great summation of golden nuggets you can take with you on your journey throughout your career or even in your own household!

This book is professionally written in expert storytelling fashion to help all of us understand that each person we meet has a part to play in the change journey. Even the person we might think has nothing to contribute can be surprisingly helpful along the way.

This book will have you laughing, crying, and cheering for the light that inevitably shines at the end of the change tunnel. You will also learn about the mistakes that happen along the way. I highly recommend that all leaders read this book. I learned so much from Donna's adventures and wisdom. I know you will too!!

Enjoy the read!

—Robin F. Anderson, SVP Commercial Card Consultant, Implementation, Service and Small Business Manager, MBA, APPM, syndicated writer and author

INTRODUCTION

A Baptist Minister and a CEO walk into a bar. The first question from the CEO is, "Hey, pastor, what are you doing in a bar?" The pastor smiles and responds, "It's the only place I won't run into my congregation." The CEO nods affirmatively, and they begin to share their woes.

CEO: "I'm trying to implement change in my financial organization. We are trying to create more of a performance environment, and nobody likes it. I'm running out of ways to get people to do things."

Minister: "Me too. I'm trying to build a stronger mission focus, but it seems our church would rather have dinner together than have people they don't know join our church. Not very biblical, but very real. I have no idea what to do to get them to move forward."

As a Southern Baptist preacher's kid and a corporate change warrior, I've looked at change from both sides now. And while they are completely different environments, there are so many similarities. Both leaders are trying to get human beings to do something different. It doesn't matter if it's opening a soup kitchen or a new bank line of business...the reasons for resistance are the same, and the emotional reactions are the same.

I remember running one corporate meeting where a man looked at me and said, "You're probably getting paid a lot more than me to run this change. So, you can make it work." I've also been in a Sunday worship service where a man stood up and asked my father mid-sermon, "Do you get paid for doing this?" My dad answered, "Yes, I do." The gentleman shuffled in place and then said, "You work for God! Why doesn't God pay you?" I'm sure the head of the treasury committee agreed, if only for a moment.

Change makes the brain uncomfortable, and it throws a little tantrum, declaring the person leading the change to be enemy number one. This means that, until success is seen, change is exhausting and requires the courageous spirit of someone willing to be yelled at, ignored, and ridiculed. Change warriors have to be girded with emotional armor, whether they are standing in front of a corporate team or a congregation.

Change is both a hot topic and a hated word, for good reasons. The idea of doing anything out of our comfort zone requires extra effort, and too many leaders seem to want a magic carpet that will float above the hard work and get them to the other side without making them unpopular or mussing their hair. They want to order change and then keep a tab on the expenses, without paying any immediate price.

Let's take it back to the bar.

CEO: "My biggest problem isn't the need for the change. Everybody agrees that the change is needed, but the managers are protecting their teams as if they are under attack."

Minister: "Well, at least you don't have to worry about your managers claiming that they've prayed about it and God agrees with them. It's hard to sponsor top down when you go to the very top, and instructions are based upon interpretation. That's really tricky. And most of my leaders won't believe in the mission approach until they see it work. And, of course, bring in money, which is challenging with missions."

There is one thing that gets in the way of successful change, and that thing has a brain, a heart and a determination to keep things the same. Human beings crave what they know because it is a survival skill. Our brain knows we survive in environments with which we are familiar; better the devil you know speaks to our left brain, which keeps us alive. And, yet, most change plans and proponents talk about engagement but include things like kick-offs and email communications without understanding how to remove the fear of that little devil we don't know.

The bottom-line is that moving people is not the same thing as moving process. It is trickier, more challenging and less predictable. It can drive a minister to a bar and a leader to distraction. It can't be tracked in spreadsheets or shown as an immediate pay-off, so it's often ignored at the cost of the change effort. Understanding behavior requires a trust in intuition, and a constant study of actions and response patterns. It isn't so much a science as it is an obsession with why and how people respond the way that they do.

I studied behavior under the tutelage of my parents who led churches through change. My mother had a master's degree, my father had two master's and a doctorate, and their approach was fascinating and successful while simultaneously painful and scary. I share these stories not to promote religion or faith, but to simply drive home my learning lessons. It just so happens my experience came from the church.

Back at the bar:

Minister: "I have tried to inspire people with some really good mission slides, but they don't seem to speak to anyone."

CEO: "No offense, but were you really inspired by those mission slides with Bob in his black socks and shorts?"

Minister: "Absolutely not. Good man, but not exactly a motivational speaker. I should have had them watch Apollo 13 instead."

CEO: "I actually had two Town Hall meetings that kicked off with a video about change. For some reason that didn't get them moving."

Minister: "No offense, but were you wearing black socks with shorts like Bob? Because that doesn't sound much better than the missionary slides."

CEO: "So, what do we do? Why aren't our messages getting through."

Why aren't messages getting through? Maybe because we are informing people rather than inspiring them. Perhaps because change is HARD and requires more than one meeting. Information alone isn't going to move anybody. I've seen companies so immersed in information they can't break through it to see a solution. Instead, they spend years addressing the same problem with different titles, they hire people who are supposed to be the "fix" who can't fix it, and they ask for more charts and graphs and research.

I am unapologetic about my willingness to use stories rather than scientific data to support my method because I have used my intuitive approach with companies that were stalled but became Fortune 100 companies once our changes took hold. I use stories because I believe in our ability to derive what we need from them. Our brains are hard-wired for story, after all. But I also believe that intuition is found in the patterns observed, in reliving the stories once we realize there is something in them that works. And it's called behavior, and it's exhibited by the people who constitute the company.

Meanwhile, back at the bar, the conversation continued.

Minister: "I was in prayer this morning, and I have a gut feeling that I need some help with this change effort, someone who can help me through the change so I can lead the church."

CEO: "And I agree. Maybe we need somebody to help us with our change story by figuring out how the heck to move these people."

And that's what I've always done. Performance has lifted and efforts have been integrated not because of my informational savvy, but because I watched a minister and his wife move a group of people on a river of faith by focusing on behavior. And I've watched leaders surpass all expectations by doing the same. The magic carpet is behavior, and it's the most challenging part of change. So don't expect any easy rides. But do expect results.

The CEO smacked the minister on the back and said, "Time to go. We have more in common than we realized." "Yes, we do," replied the minister. "Thanks for the conversation. Maybe what we just did here is what we need to do more of with our leaders. That could be a starting point."

And the CEO and Baptist minister walked out of the bar.

CHAPTER 1
FIRST YOU MUST KNOW
WITHOUT KNOWING

My family stood in a circle gazing at the pathetic sight that was our dinner. We had gone camping, which was a ritual when dad had been called to another church. Whenever there was a decision to be made, my city-born-and-bred father went to the forest, which was an interesting choice since he wasn't exactly Bear Grylls. This was the same man who saw his first small snake and asked my mother if worms had teeth.

On this particular day, he decided that we would combine the potential call to a church in California with a lesson on how to catch our own dinner and fry it up in a pan. It started with a trip to a minnow farm, which I had hoped would have chickens and haystacks and cows. Instead, we were faced first by the stench of a swimming pool crammed with little fish. It's ironic that we even tried casting our lines since we could have just leaned down and scooped up the fish.

Once the bait was secured, we proceeded to the pool next door which contained bass. Again, the bass were crammed together in a way that stunted their growth. I threw my line in but hated the thrill of the catch. I felt they were just monkeys in a barrel, and I was sure if I'd picked one up out of the water, there would be twenty-five or more hanging off of it.

But we fished for Dad, and caught about five of those suckers which Dad felt was the perfect amount for supper. We'd each get a bass, which sounded a lot better than it proved out.

Although dad liked the idea of the wild, our campsites were often a cross between nature and a 7-Eleven convenience store. Dad fired up the grill located in the campsite and proceeded to show us how to scale a fish with his Swiss army knife. This ended up being a much more brutal display than he planned since the knife obtained from some Christian vendor was a little dull. He hacked at those tiny little bodies like Jeffrey Dahmer, eliminating our appetites in the process.

He tried to debone the fish, but that proved impossible without tiny little tweezers, which his Swiss army knife did not include. So, he threw them on the grill, bones and all. The remaining carcasses were so small at this point the fish just dropped through the grill on the charcoal, and we sighed with tremendous relief.

Although we really wanted to pray for a better meal, we knew that we had gone camping with the sole purpose of praying about Dad's new opportunity. Dad was being called to a church in Southern California, and our decision-making modus-operandi always included a prayer offered in the stillness of nature. We would join hands, get quiet, and wait to see how we felt about the move.

I remember the smell of pine, the warmth of the sun, the buzz of the flies, the large smell coming from the small bass, and the power of meditative silence. I also remember opening my eyes when I heard something that sounded like a snake moving through the pine needles. If the result ended up being a snake, it would not be a good sign.

And once the prayer was over, and our hands dropped, we would all walk back to our Nimrod tent camper with a sense of peace and guidance. I remember that for every move we all got the same feeling, a "yes" on the move, except for once when my mom did not agree. This ended up being our most difficult experience as a family and as a church. While the church needed guidance, there were so many challenges within the congregants and the neighborhood, our energy was zapped on a daily basis. The church had an evangelical minister who brought in a lot of money and avoided the heroin addicts and mentally challenged adults housed in slumlord housing. He played to the wealthier members, and created a church membership whose greatest joy was giving him gifts. Dad's mission approach had never been more relevant, but it was the last thing those congregants wanted to deal with. When you have heroin addicts and young prostitutes coming to church, they kind of killed the "we're wealthy because God likes us best" buzz. Along the way, we met some of our dearest friends, but it was beyond exhausting. We stayed until prayers said it was time to go.

This was my introduction to intuition, to following the gut whether accessed by prayer or meditation or simply a sense that something was right. Of course, I didn't know all of this at such a young age. I was mostly relieved that the prayer was done and now we could swim at the pool that probably contained more urine than chlorine.

The change warrior role my parents played tended to move from start to completion in about three years, so we had a lot of intuitive moments in the woods over the years. When people hear that I moved that often they always ask if my dad was in the military, and I resist the urge to make them uncomfortable by saying something corny like, "Well, my dad was in God's Army." Instead, I tell them the truth—my parents were change warriors, and the prayer was just the beginning of our journey. We went into churches that had fallen apart for some reason and we worked, as a family, to rebuild them.

Why would a church need a change warrior? The same reason any corporation needs a change warrior; they are facing an obstacle or initiative that has required them to do things differently so they can survive and thrive. Companies and churches face the same destructive issues, including unethical behavior, financial challenges, fear of change, lack of trust, and apathy, to name a few.

Our experience seemed to involve following one particularly charismatic minister who had a bad habit of stealing money and the church secretary within the first few years of his ministry. We had to first rebuild trust with those churches by exhibiting authentic behavior and commitment to our mission. This took time and required that Dad and Mom reveal their willingness to visit congregation members, work tirelessly by teaching Sunday School and joining the choir, and deliver messages that were consistent with their leadership goals. For exam- ple, Dad had stated our commitment to missions. He backed this up by delivering sermons at a sister hispanic church once a month, and housing visiting missionaries in our home. In churches where funds had been misused or taken, Dad had to be careful when it came to raises or expenses. He had to show that he would spend their money ethically and responsibly before attempting to spend them on a new sanctuary or even choir robes. These were Baptist churches where income depended on what showed up in the morning plate, and when a previous pastor pocketed the plate money it took a while to rebuild trust. We really couldn't do much, however, about the church secretary except replace her with somebody significantly less attractive.

My parents knew that whatever their big change plan was, it would have to be executed through the members of the church. As Scott Peck says in *People of the Lie*, churches house the best and the worst of us. Change is not easy, and sometimes the change warrior must be strong enough to keep passion going even when it's not felt by everyone. Therefore, there has to be passion behind change and a belief that the need for it is somehow bigger than you are.

Our passion came from an intuitive belief that we were supposed to come to that church, no matter how difficult. But explaining that intuition to others, getting them to believe the way we believed, was a different process. Intuition has to be felt to be believed, and for those who believed only in what they could see, taste, hear or touch, this was a challenge. Sensors, as they are described in Myers-Briggs, have faith in what has been proven, not what is "felt," and make up approximately 70% of the overall population. Dad had to enroll them without absolute proof that it would work, which required taking away the "nos" by enrolling people first who believed in the possibility of his vision.

CHANGE LESSONS

A gut feeling is hard to explain.

Whether you call it inspiration, intuition, prayer or instinct, it will give you an initial "feel" when making decisions about a change. While not always on target, intuition gives you direction. Filling your brain with information containing pros and cons lists overwhelms it, which is what we call analysis paralysis. There's so much information the brain fears it will make the wrong choice, which generates anxiety. The stress freezes the ability of the collective mind to make a reasonable decision. Listen to your body. Go somewhere quiet. Life is composed of energy —make sure you know the direction your energy is going.

Passion is an essential ingredient to change.

Change is exhausting, and there will be times when the passion of the change warrior is the only thing keeping the effort alive. Therefore, the driver of change has to feel to their very core that the decision is the right one. From there comes the commitment.

Dad and Mom knew that they would enter a church that was

wounded and surviving, but they would leave it healthy and thriving. The effort in between those points would require their total heart and energy.

"Intuition is seeing with the soul." –Dean Koontz

CHAPTER 2
DENIAL ROCKS

There is relief once the change decision is made, but that is only the beginning. There is a place right after a decision is made called "buyer's remorse." This is the result of a variety of factors, but it is inevitable. No matter how much better the new opportunity is, there is a comfort zone that must be severed, and the ego will fight that break-up with every negative story it can muster. It could be as small as buying a new car, getting into it at the dealership, and suddenly missing the faded interior and comfort of the old car. Or it could be as big as leaving people you've invested in, loved, and who have supported you through thick and thin over several years.

Once my family had our gut-feeling validated through our time in the woods, Dad had to let the current church know that we were moving on. The situation had improved. We left once the choir loft was full, the Sunday School attendance numbers were back up, and Dad had gotten a raise. We finally had newer clothes and better haircuts (instead of my mom cutting our bangs so short our foreheads needed their own zip code), and then it was time to go. And we weren't leaving behind an old car, we were leaving behind friends who had cried with us, laughed with us and danced at our house (we were a house of musicians) even though we were Baptist. We were leaving those courageous, loving friends behind, along with a few others.

Dad's announcement was always emotional. He would share that our family felt God was calling us to another church that needed help, which our friends understood. They knew Dad saw churches as hospitals and he wanted to change the ones in the most pain. But all the congregation heard in his speech was that he was leaving them just as they were showing how good their church could be. He was abandoning ship, punishing them for working so hard to turn that same ship.

And there were tears of sorrow from those friends, tears of anger from those who felt betrayed, and tears of joy from those who had wanted us to leave since we walked through the doors. And standing directly behind the tears, waiting to replace them, were some fairly painful behaviors that we would get to face for the next few weeks.

While intuition can be used as a catalyst, the process of change shifts from announcement to denial to anger to grieving quickly. After Dad announced we were leaving, some would immediately cut us off and get involved in finding our replacement. They would talk to people around us and avoid eye contact when just last week we were invited to dinner at their home. While I always preferred not to have to go to dinner after a long Sunday morning, it was still painful. Leaving any job sometimes makes you invisible.

Then there were those friends who had been incredibly supportive during the toughest times, and, like Dorothy with the Scarecrow, we knew we would miss them most of all. So, we took advantage of denial. We planned sleepovers with our best friends and daily meals where laughter ruled as we relived the funniest top ten church moments.

Once everyone left, we would start to pack. We figured treating that time as if we were not really leaving was the only way to get through the emotion. We dove into the lake of denial and simply viewed it as some free time where we could clean the house, box some things up and have fun.

And we needed that moment because the next thing we would do is load up the U-Haul, pile in the car and wave goodbye to our friends who showed up to watch us leave. We hugged them while sobbing, and then had to look in the rear window and watch them get smaller and smaller. The denial wore off for all of us, and the pain set in due to the separation from everything that we knew. No matter how difficult a situation is, walking away from it is discombobulating. It makes us feel lost, alone, and a little terrified.

CHANGE LESSONS

A gut feeling can't stop denial.

The brain ignites fear messages when something unfamiliar comes your way. Even if intuition serves as a catalyst for the initial decision, the body will mentally numb you into a state of denial. Until you actually step fully into change, and let go of a secure situation and begin to fall into the new journey, denial will keep you numb. Like physical shock, it keeps you from feeling pain. And that works for a brief period, making you believe that somehow you avoided the fear, the heartbreak and the battle of change. You believe that it is absolutely true until it no longer is.

Pain is inevitable, it has a purpose, and it has to be expected.

Following your denial "bliss," change will eventually require separation from your comfort zone. You must face the things you loved most about what you're leaving, and embrace it one more time. Then, you have to push it away, feel the air between you, release the grasp, and fall into an unknown. What is waving goodbye to you will even appear better than it actually was. Because "new" doesn't contain instructions, it will require your brain to forge new neural pathways and your emotions to find ways to make it through the change. Your intuition will get quiet as the journey begins, and you will have to keep replaying the fact that something told you this move was the right move. And you'll hold on to that, and question it, and get mad at it and blame it until you are ready to face it.

"True intelligence is to rise above thinking as the source of all intelligence." –Eckhart Tolle

CHAPTER 3

U-HAULS AND THE IN-BETWEEN PLACE

The literal and figurative journey of the minister's family was a fertile learning environment. Every day was an opportunity to watch people move mountains with their faith or use it as a cross before the vampire of change. Many make church their comfort zone, their place where everything stays the same while the white water of life swirls around them. On the solid rock of faith they stand, all other stuff is sinking sand. So, when a change warrior starts hammering at that rock, there is panic because it feels overwhelming, big and threatening. And just making that change is something that causes people to question their beliefs.

The problem is that rocks are mostly immovable. Only the flow of water can change their shape. We learned that when we face change we must have a willingness to keep moving, both physically and mentally. We have to be more water than rock.

My family was always in both mental and physical motion. And nothing represented that more than the period after denial. We knew that we had to truly rev our engines by having some fun before we entered the doors of the next church, because when you are willing to challenge any comfort zone, resistance is the brain's natural reaction.

And just make that change something that causes people to question their beliefs.

We knew what was coming, and we knew that the space of time between the two churches was the only time that would be truly ours. We would see our dad more in two weeks than we had the past three years. We would sing and dance and pack and unpack, and it would be just our family. The five musketeers, leaving one adventure and moving to another. For a brief moment, there was nobody angry because we were leaving or anticipating that we would meet all their needs. We had time together.

The beginning of a move meant we got to enter that magical place in between leaving the church where you are and arriving at the church to which you are traveling. For us, the in-between place was filled with a little moving money, a father filled with the joy of possibility, and a mother who was using her skills to organize a move rather than being stuck with three kids and no car. Every change warrior needs that space because you need some time to focus on yourself and reenergize. The sheer exhaustion of change requires a temporary reprieve.

The yard sales would allow us enough money to eat out at least once at IHOP. I remember one night when Mom and Dad were packing until the wee hours, and we were suddenly awakened at 2:00 a.m. to go to IHOP because Mom was craving pancakes. Going in our pajamas and sliding into that orange booth while Mom and Dad laughed with the exhaustion and freedom of a move made IHOP one of our favorite places. Other than seeing change come out the other side, there is no greater moment than those few weeks between churches when our family was filled with love, laughter, imagination and possibility.

Only once did our journey challenge the energy needed. We were moving from Southern to Northern California and had to use a U-Haul to make the trip. The "moving package" of the troubled churches we moved to usually included the offering of the minister of music and one youth to drive down and help you pack along with enough money for a U-Haul. Ours came with a dolly that must have come from a local grocery store cart since the right wheel had a mind of its own. Since the loading of heavy furniture was done by a few church volunteers from the church we were leaving, the process was awkward because it took an inordinate amount of time, and probably funded chiropractors in the area for years to come.

Once everything was loaded up, we cried our final goodbyes to the volunteers lying in pools of sweat in the driveway. The tears were plentiful, and there were lots of promises about writing and calling for years which would turn into one to two letters, but there was also a certain peace in knowing it was time to move on. My dad and the new minister of music jumped up into the U-Haul while my mom, sister, brother, and Mitzie (our dog) jumped in the car. I was mad because I wanted to be in the very cool U-Haul. But in about an hour or so, I would be happy I was in the car.

The large U-Haul truck had a trailer attached to it with our piano and dining room furniture. While driving behind the U-Haul, mom noticed that it was leaning to the right. Then Dad and the minister of music (let's call him Dave) pulled off the road. The tire was flat, but luckily a friendly stranger offered to go find a phone and call AAA, the motor club, for us (pre-cell phone days) after a mere hour and a half, we were ready to roll.

Dad and Dave got back into the U-Haul truck with a fresh new tire. Did I mention that Dave had a prosthetic left eye? I remembered this fact not only from this trip, but also because he used to always sing "His Eye is On the Sparrow" and look up to the sky, and it became a family story. Anyway, we were cruising through Bakersfield, which you want to do at as high a speed as possible due to the excessive heat, when we noticed sparks coming from the bottom of the trailer. My mom sped up to get next to the trailer to see what was happening, when to our despair we noticed the legs of our piano were scraping along the highway.

The bottom of the U-Haul trailer had fallen out and our piano legs looked like Fred Flinstone's legs running along the road. Envisioning the truck bursting into flames, we accelerated so we could get the attention of Dave who was driving the truck. Unfortunately, his left glass eye meant he couldn't see anything on his left side. Mom slammed on the horn repeatedly. Unfortunately, Dad is deaf in his left ear, so the entire event seemed like something existential until Dave heard us and pulled over.

Dad volunteered to take the car and find a gas station that had U-Hauls available. Since we were in Bakersfield, none of us felt optimistic, but we were in motion so we started unloading the current U-Haul trailer. We thanked God that our piano had wheels, and pulled everything else off one item at a time. Dad got back with the great news that there weren't any U-Hauls at the gas station he found, but the gas station owner knew a guy who knew a guy and promised we should have a new trailer any moment. The temperature was about 110 degrees, and we looked around and noticed that we were parked near a bee farm. My mother handled many crises in the family and the church, but put a bee anywhere near her and all composure was lost. We realized there would be a dire need to keep her preoccupied.

Luckily the trailer stash included our Rawgahide lounge chairs (by the way, "Rawgahide" was a term in the 70s that showed we thought plastic was very cool) and Mom had stashed a very large bag of M&M's along with a Coleman thermos filled with iced tea.

So, we lounged on the side of the highway, swatted bees and tested the true "melts in your mouth, not in your hand" aspect of M&M's. For your information, the advertisement was correct if you consider only the chocolate. The color on the outside shell of the M&M's melted until we all had tie-dye hands. But, true to the nature of anyone who survives the ministry, we turned it into a good time. We sang hymns and praise songs like "Give me Oil in my Lamp, Keep me Burning Burning Burning," which we found hilarious since we were sweltering and stuck to our pleather chairs. While Dave played the piano, we sang, and as people passed by with their windows down they would wave and honk their horns. Amazingly, not one person stopped to see if we needed help. It was California in the early 70s after all; they probably thought it was some new form of performance art.

Several hours later, our new U-Haul trainer arrived. By that time we were sunburned, sweaty, and no longer nearly as joyous as we were when we started. A few bees had found their way over to us, and Mom didn't even have the energy to scream and run. We still had four hours on the road, so we piled in, grateful for the fact that most of the bees minded their own business, and the U-Haul guy helped us put our furniture back on the trailer.

Our moving travel days provided us with the deep, emotional breaths we needed to prepare for our next change initiative. We laughed, we planned, and we prepared so that our energy was high when we walked through the doors of the new church. We were a bit like a Broadway show that ran for three years. One curtain went down, while another was raised. And we walked in with expectations of experienced change warriors. We knew there would be two standing ovations—one when we entered, and one when we left.

CHANGE LESSONS

Change requires self-care.

Change is never easy and will take every ounce of your energy. Therefore, take some in-between time to prepare your soul for the upcoming journey. Take a short vacation from work, even if it's only for a few days. Find some time to go to Barnes & Noble and plan your initial assessment. Spend more time with those you love and allow yourself to be fully present with them. Laugh, share stories and see how you can help them. Go outside, take walks, run, jump on your Peloton, watch reruns, get a new hairstyle, buy a new outfit—do whatever you need to rest. You will need this time to enter the next journey with enthusiasm.

In-between time requires some powerful intuition.

In the land between, there is a powerful existence that is based on absolutely no data. You are between trapezes, having let go of one without a clear understanding of when or if you will catch the next. In the time between, you will have to fight the desire to control your future. You'll want to buy organizers, put up specific goals and over prepare for what's coming. But we make plans, and the universe breaks our U-Haul trailer. We look for an epiphany, a guarantee, a spark of inspiration, only to find that the sparks coming from our piano legs which are dragging along the highway. There are no guarantees that we have made the right move. There are no big voices in Bakersfield assuring us of success, only bees making us question the entire trip. The best we can do is get quiet, ask our body to remind us why we're doing this, and feel, in our gut, that the road we're traveling is the right one.

"Any real change implies the breakup of the world as one has always known it, the loss of all that gave one an identity, the end of safety."
—James Baldwin

CHAPTER 4
MAKE A HUMBLE ENTRANCE

I n the beginning, change can be addictive. Fresh out of your in-between vacation, you are rested and falsely confident. Your intuitive hunch and thoroughly reasoned decision are buoyed by the sense of relief found in finally cutting the ties to the previous place of employment, marriage, or automobile. There is nothing but opportunity and no proof that your decision is anything but brilliant. You carry your new opportunity inside of your new folder held by your relaxed hand. Everything is pretty and organized and sparkling with possibility.

Once the move was made, we were energized and renewed. Now that we had finally arrived, it was time to meet our new congregation. This was the kick-off to our "honeymoon" period, when everyone believes you are the answer they've been looking for and nobody is yet uncomfortable. Change warriors have these moments, when everyone vies for their attention and believes their savior has entered the room.

Most of our initial encounters occurred not on a formal Sunday morning, but during a Wednesday night potluck dinner. These meals provide a high for those who enjoy gambling on the roulette wheel. Imagine a wheel with "meatloaf" or "brownies" or "green beans" in place of the black and red numbers. Toss in that ball, and the odds were pretty high that it would end up on side dishes like salad or deviled eggs. However, only the serious gamblers put any money on dishes involving meat, since they were more expensive and required exquisite timing from working parents.

One Wednesday night, however, defied the odds. Several of us had been involved in drama group and choir practice since 5:00 p.m. We hadn't eaten since lunch at school and ran over to the table of food, seeking out something like macaroni and cheese or cake or cupcakes to satiate our hunger.

When we got to the table, what we saw cried "fowl". Lying upon the paper tablecloth was baked chicken, fried chicken, roasted chicken and rather raw chicken from a church member. There were over ten dishes containing nothing but chicken. There was not a casserole or a vegetable or a dessert to be found. Just chicken. I stood with all of the adults who were laughing. I wasn't amused because I was hungry. There was no real solution so we joined hands where we said an insincere prayer of thanks and dug in. We might have invented the very first protein diet.

On the Wednesday night of our introduction, there was not enough familiarity to laugh together. We knew that the core families would be present, sitting at their tables with smiles that hid the silent battle of who gets to the pastor first. As we entered the room, all talking ceased and all eyes were upon us. It's a nerve-wracking moment for a pre-teen who realizes their acne and outfit are being quickly and fiercely reviewed. The worst of it was from the core families because they were checking us out, and they had the money and influence.

The core members are there when the doors open, and will be there if and when the doors close. Believe me; the "core" represents the best and the worst of your church congregation or organizational team. Their influence is valued and their currency, whether monetary or longevity or relationship to the boss, is powerful. In our experience, every table every Wednesday had an invisible seating chart for each core family. Some would actually ask visitors to move if they had unknowingly taken their seats. Core families are the foundation of your organization, and every argument and every battle fought at Wednesday night business meetings, whether over the budget or an interim minister of music, will reveal the core families at the heart of it. They are the informal influencers, and they can be your greatest champions or your most painful obstacles.

While some core families are agile and willing to accept change, others are more fearful of it and have spent several generations making sure it doesn't touch their church. Note that people define "change" as anything that doesn't support their ideas; if they're for it, then it's progress. That's true in churches or boardrooms. From a change warrior perspective, some of these influencers will be life-long friends, but others are "rotten to the core." They await your entrance, ready with a plan to make sure you're gone in a couple of years if you upset their apple cart.

So, we walked in checking out the crowd as much as they were checking out the new minister's family. We went with our intuition on high, watching body language and understanding that the church members would decide in a matter of minutes if they liked us or not. Research shows that jury members decide the guilt or innocence of a defendant within the first seven minutes of the trial and that decision almost never changes no matter the length of the trial.

The change warrior entrance is critical to those who will be impacted by your work. They're weighing every step and every word. My parents understood that their job was to strengthen a church's present and future, not to change everything that had been done before, but people didn't know that at the entrance. There was no measure for how big the changes might be, or how much that new leader might invalidate what had been done by the leader before them.

I was taught that invalidation of the past leader is a tool used by those who have nothing new to bring to the table. Perhaps they are inexperienced or have been given a position too big for their expertise. Regardless, there was never respect for those leaders who spent time rolling their eyes at the previous leader or complaining about their actions. And we listened carefully to those who, on their first introduction to us, spent time saying how thrilled they were to have us on board because the last minister was such a disaster. We knew that person would say the same thing about us when we left.

My parents paid special attention to people's body language on that entrance, as it set up a behavioral roadmap for them to follow. Some people wore smiles that looked as if they were drawn on by a frantic artist. Others didn't hide their disdain and whispered things loudly to others at their table like, "they dressed a little casual for church, don't you think?"

Generally, though, people outside of the core families were just curious. And my parents taught us to establish comfort quickly by smiling, making eye contact, and establishing some commonality. Mom and Dad made sure that they visited every table and shook hands with all who were present. Our family told stories about our travels to establish our humanity and asked others about their lives to show our interest in them.

Most of all, my family tried to make people laugh. Laughter releases tension and puts everyone at ease. Seeing a family dressed casually let them know we weren't there to establish power, we just wanted to get to know them. In one particular instance, our clothes were packed with our furniture that was showing up several days later than expected. Since we didn't have the time to purchase anything else, we ended up making our Wednesday night entrance in the same wrinkled clothes we'd been traveling in for the past eight hours.

As we walked in, there were a lot of up and down surveys made by the snootiest members. I think a few glared at us when we walked in because they thought we were a homeless family looking for shelter. This became one of the attitudes that my dad, as a change warrior, would soon address.

But for this night, there was enough fear in the room without a dramatic entrance. By watching my parents, I learned that we should never build drama with our entrance. Instead, we should attempt to build trust because the drama will come soon enough.

CHANGE LESSONS

Honeymoons are important but fleeting.

Change warriors need to absorb the positive energy emanated with a new leader of any kind. There is universal hope that the change warrior will want what is wanted by the individual staring at them. Not yet has there been a disagreement or moment of discomfort. So, relish it, but stay alert. Every church and organization has a couple of influencers and power players who have been there before you and will be there long after. They are rarely the leaders who move on to other opportunities; instead, they stay for as long as they are allowed and poison the well to maintain their control. The honeymoon period has to be entered humbly, with a focus on those in the room who are afraid, who miss the previous leader and who want to know what every person impacted by change wonders—"What is going to happen to me?" Find a way to make an informal entrance that is focused on connecting and listening. Make no promises and forge no relationships.

Have intuition on high alert.

Watch body language carefully as you walk through the door. Some will be smiling and making eye contact, attempting to make you feel welcome. Others will be making eye contact with a hesitant smile, leaning over to someone close to them whispering something. They tend to be the ones who are more fearful. But pay special attention to those who immediately engage you in conversation about all of the problems of the last leader, who keep saying, "We're so glad you're here," and who let you know that they were part of the committee that called you. They're letting you know that you owe them and that if you do not listen to their advice, you'll be out the door like the last leader. Most of all, be kind. Listen. And know that you have plenty of time to make people uncomfortable.

"Everything is connected...no one thing can change by itself." –Peter Hawken

CHAPTER 5
DON'T REFUSE THE POUNDING

The beauty of community is that regardless of where you land, they want to feed you. In the church world, they provide a pounding.

For those of you that are not familiar with this term, a "pounding" is not as violent as it sounds. "Poundings" involve filling your pantry with food and were created in times when homes needed staple foods like flour, sugar and canned goods. Granted, we were only five minutes from the closest grocery store and didn't have to hitch up the mare to go to town in the 1970's, but the tradition continued. And I have to say, opening a kitchen cabinet and seeing lots of food creates a sense of security during a time when we felt anything but secure.

So, we celebrated the pounding. We walked into whatever home was being offered with the knowledge that there would be paper plates, plastic forks and canned foods in our cabinets and milk in our refrigerator. Minister's families are lucky this way—we have a pre-planned community ready to open their homes and cabinets.

Traditions are a beautiful thing when honored because they provide discoveries and patterns of behavior. For example, we discovered that the wealthiest members in the church gave the crappiest food. We found this out because there was always a dear friend we would make that, at some point, would state that while the single mom of two, who had nothing, provided milk and butter, the Stallworths, who own the largest realty company in the area, gave a can of yellow waxed beans. I have never confirmed what a yellow waxed bean is nor what it tastes like. That can would be left in our cabinet, ready for the next minister's family when we moved away.

We were grateful no matter what we received, which included things other people wanted cleared out of their pantry, such as expired items or half a bag of powdered milk. But we also had an idea of who was willing to financially support the church, and it often ended up not being the wealthiest. They worked hard, but basically had the opinion that dad opted for a job in the ministry that he knew wouldn't pay well so they didn't need to raise his salary. His choice, not their problem. Those who had the least to give often gave food they couldn't sacrifice because they knew what being hungry felt like.Their experience provided a deeper compassion.

Whatever the food given, a pounding makes you feel welcome. This church was accepting us by making us part of their tradition. It is proven that children feel more secure in a home where the coffers are full, where food is always available. And walking into a home with cabinets and refrigerator that are at least partially filled by people who cared enough to collect the food, come into your house, and fill your cupboards makes you feel satiated and at peace. We never ate the yellow wax beans, but once our popularity waned a little, we would gaze at the can and remember a time when being "pounded" had a different, gentler meaning.

My parents always understood that every church had a past that they were a) proud of, b) had learned from, and c) had built upon. We were to be grateful for past traditions and honored them. They had no interest in slamming the previous minister, or the traditions in place. There is something I've seen done, repeatedly, by weak leaders. They come into a job and immediately roll their eyes at what's been done in the past by the previous leader. They blow up traditions by creating new ones and declaring the old ones "outdated." Then, once they've demoralized the past enough, they fill it with people they've known from other companies who make them the most comfortable.

When I see a leader begin by invalidation, I know the company is in trouble. They will get the two-year honeymoon period, but they will not have dramatic results or make a big difference because they are not top performers. Top performers don't need to tear down to build up. They believe in people, and while they might make their own changes, they are well thought-through and carefully implemented with respect for the past in every step.

Strong leaders know that they need to review what's been done, follow the roots beneath it, and hold onto what has worked or slightly tweak things that need updating but, at root level, hold the company upright. Pay attention to how companies use change; if they are implementing change as a way to either boost profits in the short-term or provide an excuse for mediocre performance, there is a problem. . And, eventually, companies will start to totter, heavy with unnecessary change foliage, with roots that are cut by every new leader. When a strong economic or cultural wind blows, they will fall.

Dad knew that even though the church needed help, there was tremendous value to be mined from the past and important traditions that should be held onto. He never underestimated the power of tradition—instead, he listened and watched and shook the cultural pan to see what nuggets remained. And, upon those nuggets, he would build the new direction. If any change wipes out all tradition, then it's not change; it's evidence of weak leadership.

CHANGE LESSONS

Accept the help.

Once the entrance is made, you have to let people do their nesting. Most human beings simply want to help in whatever way they can, and refusal of that help could ensure that you become a foreign body that will soon be rejected. I see this with consulting companies who come in, set up a conference room, roll in with two of their strongest leaders, then send in five to seven young people right out of school to conduct interviews and somehow assess culture, all without leaving the conference room. Any leader needs to assess the culture by letting the culture welcome them in.

Value the tradition.

A tradition comes from a place of cultural value and when repeated, creates a sense of security. Traditions provide corporate identity. Today's change efforts have become too fond of blowing up the past, of assuming traditions are outdated and ridiculous. Tradition is the gift they share, and the cultural baton that says, "This has always been important to us, and we want to pass it on to you so you can become one of us."

By accepting at least some of these traditions, a change warrior lets them know that they are there to make a positive difference, and aren't positioning themselves as the knight in shining armor that saves the less than adequate. In addition, they're showing respect for the past and those who worked hard to build it. New leaders too often mock the past or are indifferent to it because they refuse to learn from those who have been there for decades. You don't have to change everything —keep the pieces and the people that have worked and build around them. If honorable, traditions should be respected and accepted graciously.

"Great changes can best be brought about under old forms." –Henry George

CHAPTER 6
THE DISAFFECTED SERVE ROAST BEEF

When we first started at a new church, early on we would be invited for dinners with different church members every Sunday. This part of the journey is referenced as the "honeymoon" period. You can see it experienced by new pastors as well as CEOs. It is a glorious transition from the introduction; a time when everybody is happy due to a lack of information. My dad knew that this was the period to build relationships and positive energy with people. A spike in optimism is going to be very necessary when people hit the next phase, which includes the dreaded yet necessary uninformed pessimism.

Those meals during the honeymoon period could be charming or a form of purgatory, depending upon the cook and the conversation. One thing we could count on, however, was that during the honeymoon period, we would almost always be served roast beef. In the day, roast beef was the fanciest home-cooked meal a household could offer a new minister. And that roast beef would be placed on the finest linen tablecloth. The same thing happens in organizations, when nice lunches are brought in for new team meetings, or new leaders are taken out to the best restaurants to be wined and dined.

While Sunday meals were appreciated, they were not eagerly anticipated by the kids, no matter what age. First of all, we were often exhausted because of late Saturday nights. In many churches, mom typed up the bulletins (basically, flyers handed out each Sunday morning with announcements and an outline of the service) on Saturday afternoon, and we had to fold them on Saturday night. This usually included a quick editing review, except for one night when we were all tired. We folded our 300 bulletins in record time, only to find out during the service the next day that instead of "Collection of Tithes and Offerings," Mom had typed "Collection of Titties and Offerings."

The Sunday meals were as much about constant conversation as anything. We were the entertainment, and often the church members who invited us over stared at us, waiting for the new leader to set the conversational boundaries. I'm pretty sure people felt if they offended the new minister while breaking bread they were one step closer to hell. To break up the discomfort, we came up with stories, and as a fairly humorous family, we got people to laugh so they could loosen up a little. All change warriors have that intuitive ability of knowing when to press and when to let up on the gas. My dad preached an entire sermon around the humor of Jesus, supporting his point that crowds would not have followed him around and people would have not left their work and families for someone who didn't ever make them laugh.

We also had unintentional moments, as I struggled my entire life with knocking things over at the dinner table...and a meal that combined dark gravy with a white tablecloth rarely ended well. Every spill was met with tense smiles of anxious hostesses who were afraid of offending the pastor's family but really wanted to throttle me.

Early on we learned that these dinners were not social gatherings, they were critical auditions. Because congregants wanted to get to know us, they were generally filled with questions that we knew could reflect either sincere interest or conversational traps. And sometimes there were unintentional tripwires.

According to my mother, there was one incident when I was four-years-old, that qualified as an audition fail. The woman serving us dinner had cooked roast beef (honeymoon), mashed potatoes and peas. I was refusing to eat my peas, starting my rebellion of all green foods at a very young age. While she was kind, this church member wasn't quite as gifted in the looks department as some, and she made the mistake of saying, "Donna, if you eat your peas you'll grow up to be a pretty young woman." I looked up at her and, with the honesty of a toddler said, "They didn't make you pretty!" Case made but never closed.

While the conversations were key, food became a type of intuitive tip off for where we were in the change process. Roast beef and linen represented the honeymoon period, which transitioned to chicken and opinions once dad's first change was suggested. As change became more significant, our lunch invitations dropped precipitously, allowing dad the gift of Sunday football but creating the dread of critiques. Once the light was seen at the end of the tunnel and the revived congregation saw change actually worked, we were invited out to steak dinners at our local steakhouse. Everything was measured in food.

My dad and mom would always listen carefully at these lunches without making promises about upcoming changes that they might not be able to keep. It's tempting to say "I understand you're not happy with the new pew arrangement in the sanctuary. Well, we don't really like it either and we're going to see what we should do about it." Then you find out that the congregational member who informally "paid" for the pews through a generous offering did it only under the agreement that they must never be moved for the duration of all eternity.

We took advantage of the relationship building opportunities offered by our roast beef lunches, but we knew that the honeymoon period would not last forever. Even as a child, you only have to go through one three year stint to remember the changes in behavior. Once real change kicked in, conversations changed, tablecloths were removed, invitations slowed down. That's when we knew Mom and Dad were making a difference. Plus, we got all slim and trim.

The beginning of a change warrior's journey is very similar to falling in love. Most of us know that the early stage of love is made up of what I call "reflection love", when our mirror neurons create a love so new that we are sure that this relationship will involve no problems, no differences, just eternal bliss.

And a change warrior begins as the love interest of everybody that's not yet affected by the change. They look at you and see, reflected, the change they've always wanted but never gotten. Battles ensue to make sure desires can be shared in intimate settings.

One woman invited us to lunch only to spend the entire afternoon discussing the color of the choir robes and why she felt they needed to be changed. She simply glowed with anticipation, sure that dad's most important action would be correcting the choir robe catastrophe that was ignored by the previous minister.

In change theory, this lovely little place people visit is also known as "uninformed optimism." Uninformed optimism means that your change has yet to be defined or affect anybody's life, so the lack of movement is misinterpreted as eternal hope. It's like when my dad said he'd consider letting me go to a party in high school and then disappeared for an hour. I had an hour filled with incredible hope, due to his lack of action. Later I realized he had forgotten the question, and when I restated it, he answered with a resounding "NO!" As I was already dressed and my friend was waiting in the driveway to take me, that was a brutal introduction to the concept.

Quick decisions during the honeymoon period are based upon a presumption that everyone will remain as happy with you as they are right now. Much like a marriage, that simply is not true. Pretty soon, the same person who greeted you with the most enthusiasm will become dissatisfied. And that's when the fun begins.

CHANGE LESSONS

Front-load on uninformed optimism.

Happy are the lunch-goers who feast on roast beast. While the honeymoon is intoxicating, every change warrior needs to be careful not to be lulled into complacency. Instead, they must understand that change has a life-cycle that starts with uninformed optimism. This stage is not to be treated as a fun ride, but is instead a time to take in questions, settle people's nerves, tell funny stories, and gather energy.

Talk to people, listen to people and let them know how much you appreciate their contributions. Take the time to get away from the work environment; there is something about a good meal outside of a conference room that makes the conversation more honest and engaging. Use your intuition, following gut-feelings about areas of concern or places you need to dig a little deeper.

Don't believe the hype.

Whenever a leader of change looks into the pond of compliments offered during the honeymoon period and believes the hype, they're going to fall into that pond and it won't be pretty. While people mean well, the compliments you're receiving from most are either because a) they think you're going to fix something for them, or b) they want to hang onto the popular person. When the popularity goes, so do they. Others are in for the long haul, but they generally offer lunch when you need it most; they become those people who rip your heart out when you have to leave. They won't fight for your attention up-front, because they aren't vying for attention. They are silently waiting to offer support.

"Every act of creation is first of all an act of destruction." —Pablo Picasso

CHAPTER 7
BE WARY OF THE CHEEK KISSERS

nformal introductions to a new church or executive team is the time used to "sniff out" the new leader. I watch this happen whenever a new dog joins the playground at a local doggy daycare. While a little more literal, it's how dogs determine if they trust the new canine, or if they should be on full alert. While these introductions are important, things get ratcheted up when introductions are formal, in the press and in the sanctuary. Because this means the deal is done, the change is here, and everything is signed and approved.

Those first Sundays when we would officially "join" the church, our family had to walk down the aisle during the altar call and be introduced to the entire congregation. We were usually seated on the first pew, so it wasn't a long walk. But turning to face the congregation, with all eyes upon you, was a nightmare for my introverted brother and sister and a jolt of extroverted electricity for me. At our last church, which also happened to be in a wealthier area, we had to be introduced before our new clothes we had bought for the occasion were delivered, and all we had was a box of old clothes that were supposed to go to Goodwill. Therefore, my fourteen year old brother had on pants that were too short and too tight, and my older sister had on a "maxi" dress with flowing sleeves that would have made a hippie proud. It worked in California, but the neckline plunged a little too deeply for the Virginia crowd, and I'm pretty sure they thought she resembled a flower child/hooker.

I was sixteen years old, and could only find a "sizzler" dress. What was a sizzler? It was a two piece garment that included a bodysuit with a skirt so short it had to match the skirt, or else you made the mistake of moving in any direction. It was blue with red whales on it, and the only shoes I had were high-heeled white sandals. I was mortified. Apparently, the teenage boys on the front row were fairly happy.

So there we stood -- our parents, two hookers and a nerd awaiting the opportunity to meet the congregation. But those moments were like paradise compared to what was coming. For once we were introduced and the benediction given, it was time for what seemed like each and every church member to come through the line to shake our hand, hug us and sometimes lay a big, wet kiss on us. In retrospect, I'm sure most people in line dreaded the wait and awkward welcomes as much as we did. But, like all experiences, this was a chance to learn. Based upon our experience, those who lined up first were either a) going to be our greatest supporters, or b) represented a core family who was already unhappy with us because the other core family liked us, and were planning our demise.

Those who ran to get in line first, who shook our hands and then held them, or leaned in for a kiss, would become the controllers. If you don't believe in the power of a kiss, think about *The Godfather*, or Judas. A kiss on the cheek doesn't always mean "welcome." Sometimes it means you have been marked and your time is limited.

Body language quickly lets you know the personality type. Kissers are willing to hold your hand and make eye contact to ensure you don't pull away. Watch for:

- Level One: They turn the handshake into a two-handed grab, pull you towards them, and act as if the kiss was mutual. Their kiss is firm, branding you as theirs.
- Level Two: The air-kissers who made you feel like you were in Hollywood but actually just didn't want to mess up their

make-up. They were too interested in themselves to put time into pushing you out.

- Level Three: The sincere kissers. They hugged you first, then gently planted one on your cheek as a welcome. It felt like family, and we'd soon find out that was exactly who they would become.

However they might plant the kiss, our intuition kicked in with every smooch—a deep sense of what was sincere, what was tentative and what was prematurely hostile. We often discussed around the lunch table who sincerely welcomed us, and who provided a mob kiss in the tradition of "a kiss on your cheek today, the head of your favorite horse in your bed tomorrow." You see, a few of the cheek kissers acted like they were potential supporters but would actually end up being our Judas. They weren't bad people, they simply felt the church belonged to them and they liked it just the way it was. Just like the Pharisees and Sadducees in the time of Christ, their job was to protect the status quo and make sure no change shook their foundation of control.

Others are truly glad to have you in place for all the right reasons. But, regardless, we were taught to be grateful for those who were there before us, and stand not in judgment but simply as people who knew our role was to move forward, not burn what was behind us.

Here's the bottom line: When you're a new change leader of any kind, use your intuition as you are introduced. If your sense is "something feels insincere here," simply remember it. Be careful. You might get to know the person and find out the sense wasn't correct, or you might discount your gut feeling to your own detriment. I had a woman who worked for me in the corporate world who felt insincere the first few days I interacted with her. I thought she had a mean streak. Then she found out that I was a mover and shaker, and suddenly we became the best of friends for years until the day that she stole all of my money. I should have followed my gut.

Trust that people are doing what they sincerely feel is right for them and their church. Trust that most people want you to succeed and are there to support you as best they can. But be careful trusting anybody who jumps in to criticize a previous leader in the first conversation. And, if they hold your hand and pull you in for the kiss on the cheek, just check under the emotional covers for a potential horse head. I'm just saying.

CHANGE LESSONS

Make sure you pack your first impression clothes.

Change warriors have to understand that the first ten seconds offer a visual impression that could either build a strong foundation for a relationship or create a need to apologize and rebuild visual trust for months to come. Make sure that you dress in a way that will communicate with your audience, not intimidate it. While intuition is usually an immediate reaction, many confuse it with the brain that is constantly sizing up the competition. How you present yourself can exhibit whether you respect the environment you are entering, or are going to cause trouble immediately. Wearing a "sizzler" is not a good idea. I didn't really have a choice, but I think I spent at least a year trying to convince some members that I wasn't "Mary Magdalene before Jesus."

Categorize your kissers.

According to Malcolm Gladwell, author of the book *Blink*, first impressions are accurate most of the time. Therefore, while you don't want to predestine relationships by judging others too quickly, body language and verbal messages in your first introduction will give you a "gut" feeling that will generally be on target. Pay attention to body language—do people shake your hand to pull you closer to themselves? Do they make eye-contact that is warm or do they offer a vampiric, soul-sucking stare? Do they smile sincerely, or are they smiling in a way that could potentially be hiding fangs? In meetings, watch for those who watch you and then quickly make eye contact with those around the table, obviously sharing some pre-meeting topic about your potential as a leader. Don't assume the quiet ones are trouble, sometimes they are taking you seriously and sizing things up. In the early stages, look for those who sincerely want to help (most of the congregation), but know that the controllers will be future obstacles to change. Watch for them, because they can be deceptively supportive, dominating your time and trying to stay close so they can go in for the bite that will make them yours, forever.

"It's the most unhappy people who most fear change."
  –Mignon McLaughlin

CHAPTER 8
FIND DISCIPLES AND DRIVE THE FORD LTD

remember one church that prided itself on giving their minister nice cars, so that he/she could represent the financial success of the church while visiting neighborhoods. This church was in a very low-income part of town filled with gangs, and there was appreciation and respect for material representation. My parents were not familiar with this type of giving, and when they presented Dad with a large, light blue Ford LTD, his response was one of confusion. Up to this point our nicest vehicle had been a white Dodge Dart that broke down every other day. My dad valued humility and created mission churches that were low on fancy and high on service. He felt that visiting people in trailer parks and barrios in an expensive car might make him look pretentious or cause them to mistake him for a pimp or drug dealer. That's not stereotyping, but an actual description of what each drove in the neighborhood. Plus, he was used to driving Toyotas, and he said that driving the LTD was like trying to steer an aircraft carrier.

So, after a few months of scraping the sides of lots of other things like our mailbox and trash cans, my dad requested in a business meeting that he trade in the LTD for a smaller car. Based upon the scowls on the faces of the congregation, we realized this was a bad move.

While Dad felt he was giving the church a financial break while better representing the role of a missions pastor, the church members took it personally. Their last pastor had LOVED the Ford LTD (along with the money he stole from the church). They thought this was something that would impress their new minister—it was a gift from the heart and, perhaps, a way to heal the past. Somehow the refusal of the gift invalidated their past and rejected their affection.

We did get a green Nova, though it was never really accepted by people in the church and was resented every time we pulled into the church on a Sunday morning. We hurt some feelings on that decision, and hurt feelings don't heal quickly. We forgot that sometimes what is a rational decision for us is actually connected to the heart of the giver.

If Dad had found those who could have their finger on the pulse of the congregation, if he had asked them for their opinion, he could have avoided the rebuilding of relationships that faced him over the next year. I don't know that he ever fully recovered. When something is tied to the heart, forgiveness is harder to find. The damage went to the very thing that kept the church functioning, that provided passion. He was preaching servant leadership but he rejected a gift from those who felt they were serving him.

During the honeymoon period, it's important for the change warrior to begin to gather together a small group of supporters that are willing to implement necessary change and make it work.

Most companies assume change happens top down with high-level executives and supervisors. It doesn't, simply because some of those high-level folks aren't on board yet. Plus, all great change happens from the inside out, with people who have their thumb on what is really happening out there, where the obstacles are, and what people really want. You need the passion of people not yet beaten down and flattened by the many responsibilities of the executives.

You also need disciples who a) believe in the change, b) can "sell" the change to colleagues, c) and are tenacious influencers. Unlike a lot of executive positions, this group is not composed of "yes" people who are in place to tell the leader how freaking amazing she is every single day. They are those willing to be honest, push back, and question, all in the name of change. Jesus himself found his group of disciples, and one in particular named Judas showed that, as a leader, he was willing to keep those who disagreed with him as part of the team.

Disciples are not just a nice-to-have during times of change, they are a have-to-have. If the change warrior is an external, they leave behind a core of people who can carry on once they are gone. So many changes are rolled-out and implemented, but never integrated, because there is a coalition of passionate souls whose very job is to ensure the change stays relevant every single day.

Disciples help you avoid missteps by giving you valuable feedback, especially during the honeymoon phase. It is critical that the change warrior understands what is important to the place they are serving and what represents more than seen by the naked eye. There are often gifts to new leaders, whether emotional or literal, and when they are not fully appreciated for what they represent, the honeymoon can end early.

Disciples could be in the form of a small team out in the field. What you need to do is drive change forward with a small group of people to show that the change will work in any key setting. More than 80% of people will refuse to jump onboard the change train until they have proof that whatever the change is actually works. Your coalition will be trained first, prepared for objections and will help create the next phase of the change roll-out. They will take away the "no's," and help build a better change process in the meantime.

Find your courageous, trusted, influential people. Put them in place, and most of all, listen to what they have to say.

CHANGE LESSONS

Find your disciples.

Change warriors need to begin looking almost immediately for those few who are influencers connected to the congregation or corporate team that is critical to the success of the change. This circle will be small. For example, if you're working with a bank that has 400 branches, you might try to find four branches that will implement your change effort the right way. This circle of supporters will be critical because they'll show that the change works. They'll take away the "no's" when others desperately want, to prove the new ideas that don't work.

Listen to those who know the ground truth.

The military has a great term called "ground truth." It means understanding what is actually going on in the field, rather than listening to the stories fed up to leaders. As a CEO once told me, "The higher up you go, the less truth you hear." Every change warrior has to be courageous enough to listen to the truth about preparation, roll-out, reactions and next steps. Too many go the safe route of providing only success stories so they can eventually wrap-up and get a pay day. Others refuse to listen because their only intent is to elongate the relationship for a better contract. The best change warriors know that having their disciples will provide ground truth and allow real-time corrections. By change warriors having these qualities, it will help surface speed bumps before they become obstacles. Disciples also help avoid a decision based on fact that will fester in the hearts of those impacted. Because once the heart distrusts the change warrior, it's a long road back.

"Changing people's customs is an even more delicate responsibility than surgery." –Edward H. Spicer

CHAPTER 9

DISCERNING BETWEEN PEBBLES AND STONES

The honeymoon phase of change can last one year or one week, depending upon the depth of the change and the speed with which you are expected to make the conversion. People don't like change, even when they requested it because when change begins to actually happen, it requires energy. The brain is building those new pathways, and unless there has been enough pain to cause the change, there could be a quick retraction of commitment. So, this first year requires a variety of short-term wins that can build confidence in the change warrior and the transition itself. While our church honeymoon usually lasted approximately one year, the amount of congregational adoration would shift slightly even within the first month as small changes started to be put into place.

We learned that you had to build enough belief initially to replace the fear that inevitably pulls people back. We needed small wins and needed them fast to take away the future "I told you it wouldn't work" comments that were waiting in the wings. The brain doesn't like change, and as only approximately 10% of team members are early adopters, you need small victories to build confidence. The first step was figuring out which changes were:

Pebbles: Low level of discomfort, small number of people impacted, creating only enough ripples to raise energy levels

Stones: High level of discomfort, large number of people impacted, which create tsunami-like ripples that could wipe out change effort before it begins

Learning from our LTD debacle, we began to conduct an informal verbal assessment (sometimes starting with those Sunday lunches) of what changes might be more easily accepted and what changes would cause some members' heads to spin. And I mean spin all the way around like Linda Blair's character in *The Exorcist*, followed by bursts of anger in business meetings that would metaphorically match the pea soup scene.

Here are the "stone" changes we learned should <u>not</u> be attempted in the honeymoon period:

New Hymnals: Congregational members love knowing that "Holy, Holy, Holy" is on page 1 of the hymnal, and "When I Survey the Wondrous Cross" is page 162. Why is this important? Because it's familiar, and it gives them a distinct advantage on Sunday night services when it's "request" night. You can always beat the guy who wants to sing another rousing rendition of "Beulah Land" if you can call out your number before he calls out his.

New Dishes: A rare business meeting that resulted in a physical altercation was not about scriptural interpretation, but about the purchase of new dishes for the fellowship hall. I guess fellowship was not at the top of everyone's mind on this particular issue. Dad mistakenly assumed this would be a surface topic, a pebble, that would cause few congregational ripples. He was wrong. The topic drew intense emotion from a couple of families, heated words were exchanged, and a couple of husbands stepped outside after the meeting for a short-lived fist-fight. Who would expect a testosterone-filled altercation would be about a topic that included the word Corningware?

Sunday Night Services: Anyone who attends church knows that Sunday nights tend to involve the same 28 people each week. After a busy Sunday morning, the thought of coming back to church at 7:00

p.m. was not popular even twenty years ago. Service topics were generally a potpourri of time fillers, like the Sunday night sing-a-long. In one church, Dad decided to discuss the elimination of Sunday nights, since few people attended, and he was exhausted at the end of the Sunday services.

When he presented his suggestion, most congregants were fine with eliminating Sunday night services. Except, of course, for the 28 people that came faithfully and apparently had nothing else to do. Dad decided to keep the service since he was accused of wanting to see the end of the then-Redskins' 4:00 p.m. televised games instead of worshiping God, which was partially true.

The very things we thought were pebbles, ended up being stones. And the stones? They couldn't be wholly revealed until we got a few small wins under our belt. Denial is a powerful thing and to try to express the big changes coming in a way that people would hear is impossible. We learned that in times of change, people can't handle the big things, refuse to acknowledge them, or don't feel in control of them and decide to move on to what they can control. Those are usually the small things.

Disciples play a big part in the small wins. If you have a new sales program for example, pilot it in a few areas with the best disciples and show others that getting increased sales is possible. Shine a relentless spotlight on the good stuff so that people's denial can slowly melt in the proof, and their belief that it can be done is gradually built. Disciples are there to introduce, train and reinforce, offering a consistent belief that it will work and surfacing anything that doesn't. If we could avoid these taboo topics in the honeymoon phase, we found that other changes could be made that would build a strong foundation for the more active period of change initiation. If these taboo topics were avoided, most of the other changes that might occur in the first year helped build an evangelistic zeal by showing that the first changes were successful and ultimately ingrained in the culture.

CHANGE LESSONS

Gain positive energy with pebbles.

Every change warrior should understand what topics are precious to their audience. These are generally repeated activities that have created a comfort zone for those who have practiced them for years. It might be the fact that retail employees aren't required to shake hands with customers, that they open at 8:35 instead of 8:30, or that they have a small coffee vendor parked out front each morning. Whatever the taboo topics are, don't undermine change before it gets started with the "stones" that will derail the effort. Instead, start with small changes that, like pebbles thrown in a pond, will create ripples of energy without significantly disrupting the status quo.

Don't underestimate the dishes.

When people are going through change, they're not going to throw fits over the big, conceptual changes. People believe what happens in front of them, not what's discussed as the final vision. For example, telling people that you are going to make client experience a new point of focus for the next year doesn't look or feel like anything different yet.

But going into a branch and taking down homemade signs they've been making for years is something they can see, touch and feel.

Every tangible item has an intangible emotion behind it—it might be that one branch used to get awards for its homemade marketing posters. Or maybe the form you're deleting was created after a year of intense meetings. So, don't underestimate items that are in front of your change audience right now and have a history behind them. People grieve over loss, and the small decisions were often theirs. Now, they are facing some change coming down the road that seems big and unknown, so they grasp their security blanket tightly and fight back.

I remember one woman who had a heart attack because we replaced the fake Christmas lilies with real ones. We had no idea why, until we dug through a lot of conversations. We discovered that when her mother passed away, she left money to the church that was used to purchase those fake Christmas lilies. Behind every protest is personal passion. Don't underestimate human feeling when making change, nor their ability to attach feeling to inanimate objects.

"Birth is violent, whether it be the birth of a child or the birth of an idea." –Marianne Williamson

CHAPTER 10
ACTION AND THE ALTAR CALL

I n the Baptist church that I was raised in, the ultimate goal of every Sunday School class and Sunday sermon was to have someone change their lives by "going down the aisle" during what is referred to as the "invitation call." Whether you go to ask for prayer, declare your faith or renew your faith, it is a very personal decision, and not to be viewed as a "win" by anyone. But any of us raised in a Baptist setting know that the number of people responding on a Sunday sets up a sense of success or failure. And a new minister who has a primary change initiative in mind understands that it's important to have more people walk down that aisle in the first year than any other time.

Nobody will admit that numbers matter at church, even though all churches I was a part of updated the Sunday School attendance numbers at the front of the sanctuary each week. And every bulletin announced new converts and members. It mattered to people to see their church grow, just as it matters to any leaders of organizations. As they say, you're either growing or you're dying. And when you're doing it all for God, there's a little extra pressure, especially when you're making church people a little unhappy. I remember when I briefly worked as a hostess at a restaurant that the majority of members would frequent after church each Sunday. Passing by tables, I would see people leaning towards each other and saying, between bites, "We are getting a lot of new members!" or "Nobody's come forward in a couple of Sundays" or "The pastor is a little off his mark with his sermons. I wish he'd preach more about..." Everyone wants to be part of an energized organization with a charismatic leader of whom they can feel proud, and the world values graphs that go up, not down.

As the preacher's daughter, I really valued the honeymoon phase of our church engagement because almost every single Sunday somebody came down that aisle. But I also had lived through the period where change had kicked in, and Dad stood at the front of that aisle all alone, ending the hymn early because it was clear no decisions were being made. That's how I developed what might be named in the future as a preacher's kid panic attack.

As soon as dad came down the stairs to stand at the front of the aisle, my heart would pound, and I would look around the sanctuary in stealth mode for any sign of movement, or listen for that lovely sound of panty-hosed thighs rubbing together as women walked down the aisle. I knew that people going down the aisle meant Dad's graph was going up and he was off the hook for another Sunday. More than that, I know it made him feel positive about this work and that in the middle of change, without people going down the aisle, he would doubt himself more and sink into some temporary despair.

Once that first person went down the aisle, even if it was to complain about how long the service was going, there was going to be another person. Here's my own informal statistics based on nothing but twenty years of observation—one person going down the aisle increases the odds of another person going down the aisle by about 80%. There's a truth to Einstein's theory that energy can only transform into another type of energy, and it is true from a motivational standpoint as well. Early adopters are critical to early stages of change, since there is a need for safety and proof, a willingness to follow but a reluctance to lead. This is true for disciples helping with change as well. Once someone within the organization declares a faith in the upcoming change, someone else is going to come down that proverbial aisle eager to be a part of something exciting. That's why you want to constantly show the number of converts, because you're putting a spotlight on success. Not only because it influences others, but because once change really kicks in, there is going to be some folks leaving the effort and potentially the building. You need the energy now to prepare for those uncomfortable moments.

For me, there was no more uncomfortable moment than watching Dad sing four verses of "Just As I Am" while tumbleweeds blew down the aisle instead of congregants. During the second phase of change when popularity was not at an all-time high, Dad could face as many as ten plus Sundays without anyone coming down the aisle. I learned that people feel more positive change when happy things are happening. However, not many line up for uncomfortable change. Apparently, God's call gets really quiet during these periods. And as the daughter of the man who spent hours at home preparing his sermon, who left the house at 5:00 a.m. and often didn't get home until 11:00 p.m. due to services, visits, weddings and funerals, it was beyond painful to watch him stand there alone.

Sometimes, I would actually ask people to go down for a prayer request just so there'd be some motion (yes, I planted them). On those Sundays when nobody came forward, there was a silence after the last verse that was heavy with disappointment. Dad would close his hymnal, the pianist would stop playing, and people would hang their heads before the benediction even started. In a Baptist church, people coming forward are like sales numbers for companies. Dad would have <u>hated</u> that analogy since he never wanted it to be about numbers. But sometimes it simply is, and change requires the energy that any "lift" provides.

Let me be perfectly clear, I do not encourage manipulative techniques like those I've seen used by some evangelists. They know how to create a false high by being loud, having energetic music and creating a frantic need for faith. I have one certain revival team branded into my brain because of one hilarious moment. The church had requested Dad's least favorite thing—a revival. And it is exactly what it sounds like, an energy surge that some believed would give lasting impact. But like most motivational seminars, the energy lasted for approximately 24 hours, until the converted went home and realized nothing else had changed, except their excitement level. The revival team my dad really wanted backed out at the last minute, so dad took the second string, which actually ended up being walk-ons that had never really played the game. We knew we were in trouble when the lead minister was a guy that briefly attended our day camp for kids at one church and hit on every girl aged fifteen and over.

Anyway, they spent Wednesday, Thursday and Friday evening torturing us with terrible sermons that had little content but lots of volume. Sunday was their big finish, although you wouldn't know it by the "fill in the blanks" sermon that was delivered and music led by a man who flailed like a drowning man during hymns, hoping no one noticed that he had no idea how to lead music. Let me put it this way —slides from the latest missionary trip to Guatemala would have been an improvement to this Sunday experience.

The evangelist knew that he could make up for a bad week with a big altar call finish. He understood that people remember the finish and are impressed with numbers. Therefore, he was determined to get people down the aisle using any manipulative tactic possible. He started with:

If you feel you need to make a change in your life, come forward and talk to me. Result: No one came forward—though a few in the back tried to slip out to the local steak house.

They didn't make it before his next instructions that were:

If you have a prayer request, come forward. Result: One person came forward.

Now, Evangelist Mike was getting nervous. We were on verse three of a four verse hymn, and he had only one taker. He upped the ante at this point:

If you have a family member that needs to know the Lord, come forward.

Result: Five people came forward, much to the chagrin of the family member who remained in the pew.

The net grew wider as he had a surge of unearned optimism:

If you have heard of someone in the news that needs prayer, come forward.
Result: Fifteen people came forward.

Momentum was being built, and he had approximately 50 more people to get down that aisle. At this point my brother, sister and I were sitting on the second pew with our mother. My sister, purely out of pity, was going to go forward by the third request. Mom looked at her with her deathly look and mouthed the word "NO." Suddenly we knew that Mom didn't appreciate manipulation for the Lord and was not going to let us move an inch.

Meanwhile, Evangelist Mike went for broke:

If you love your family, come forward now to pray for them. Result: Thirty people came forward.

If you love the Lord, come forward now to tell him. Result: Everybody else came forward, minus the preacher's family, and those unsaved family members.

We stood there, rigidly, with my mom passing pinches down the pew deterring any forward movement. Evangelist Mike glared directly at us, and Dad looked out the back stained glass window slightly over our heads, realizing Mom was not going to move. Determined to get the pews cleared, Evangelist Mike gave it one more shot:

If you love this church and your pastor, come forward.

It was like High Noon. Evangelist Mike glared at my mom, and she glared back. My brother, sister and I were trying to hold back laughter at the absurdity and tears of embarrassment at the same time. The entire congregation was at the front of the church staring at us. We finally looked up, proud that we weren't going to give into an insincere altar call. The red-faced, contorted rage displayed on Evangelist Mike's face declared that we were victorious. He finally boomed a rather violent benediction, and we all went home.

Any leader with integrity understands that there should be a natural lift in energy during the first phase of change. Small successes can be highlighted, but they will primarily be behavioral, not numerical. Those claiming big lifts, especially in the first few weeks, are bad evangelists at heart because they're moving numbers around to create a faux lift that very few will buy into, but most will stand by. The challenge with praising behavioral lift is that too often during times of change, the specific behaviors desired are not ever defined. Instead, numbers are discussed, numerical goals are set and there's absolutely no roadmap that will honestly drive the results.

Real change leaders set behavioral goals, provide the disciples to role-model and drive those behaviors while setting up a way to spotlight them when they happen. They know that the lift will come once the right behaviors have been in place and reinforced. Rather than coercing converts and manipulating the numbers, they believe that what people do actually drives results. And, eventually the right leaders will shine. By the way, the leaders who shine during times of change might not be the usual "golden" leaders. Why? Because the specific goals defined means the greatest story doesn't win, and the manipulators will be found out.

CHANGE LESSONS

Measurement matters.

As change starts turning into action, there has to be some clear expectations. No matter the environment or change that occurs, there have to be specific behaviors that are determined to achieve the desired numerical results. People trust trends, like to follow lines and will jump in line once they see things going the right direction. No one likes to jump onboard the Titanic. We learned that lesson the hard way. So, in any change, know that you have to first look at your desired lift and start communicating the right behaviors. Because, I promise you, those who start acting first will get the first lift.

Showcase what people are doing right.

As a change warrior, you have to ensure that there are steady successes in your first phase that are showcased and discussed. As often as possible, show charts with the red line going up—because you're going to have plenty of time when that climb won't be as steep. The discomfort of change means we're anxious to go back to the comfort zone as soon as any "problem" arises. Furthermore, make sure your "disciples" are getting and communicating their wins so you can take away the "no's" delivered by your skeptics. The more wins you can report, the more people go down the aisle, the greater momentum your change will garner.

Gain followers while the energy is good.

Human nature shows that people follow other people. Your "early adopters" are usually less than 10% of your population, and that mass in the middle shifts direction, following energy. While the going is good, get as many people on board as possible. People "bandwagon" by nature; they want to know that if they are making a decision others are making. That's why one of the most brilliant things McDonalds did in the 60's and 70's was post how many hamburgers had been sold. Who wouldn't eat at a restaurant chosen by least 10 billion other diners? Get results while people feel safe. When more people emotionally show support and jump , this will increase the amount of people jumping on board because they feel safe in their decision.

> *"It's not so much that we're afraid of change or so in love with the old ways, but it's that place in between that we fear...it's like being in between trapezes." –Marilyn Ferguson*

CHAPTER 11
POSITIVE ENERGY - AVOIDING THE PRAYER BENCH

While the altar call creates positive association (the joy of a new member, a conversion, etc.), the prayer bench does exactly the opposite. For those of you who are not familiar with a prayer bench, it's exactly as described. Only one of our churches had prayer benches, facing the pulpit. From the back of the sanctuary you would see the elevated pulpit with two sets of stairs coming down the left and right. At the bottom of the stairs, on either side of the Lord's Supper table (also known as the Communion table for non-Southern Baptists) were two benches, one on the left of the table and one on the right. In this particular church, the benches could be viewed by anybody in the church. The purpose of the benches was to provide a secure place to kneel for those who wanted to pray during the altar call.

During change, every organization has a time period where things seem to be working, and numbers are lifting. It's a glorious time, filled with uninformed optimism that the tough part has been avoided and all is right with the future. Then real change starts happening, and the answers aren't found because an unknown has been entered. The mantra of early change is *We've not done this before or at least in this way, and we're not sure exactly what to do next.* That's when leaders get quiet, and a few are probably driven to their proverbial knees in hopes of finding an answer somewhere.

While the intention of the prayer bench was to provide a humble position to silently ask for help, it tended to attract those who wanted every person in the congregation to witness their pain. And that always threw a wrench into the positive association we were trying to spotlight.

The prayer bench people were few but powerful. After observing for months, I decided that these were the people who left the service to use the bathroom every single Sunday, yet inevitably sat on the front pew so we could all watch them sashay in and out while Dad tried to preach. They were the emotional exhibitionists, anxious to let everyone in the church know how incredibly hard their lives were.

Change brings out either the best of us or the neediest of us; those in the middle just wait silently to see which way the wind is going to blow. Change brings an opportunity to be seen and heard, so often the needy raise their hands to be a part of the initial effort, when their only real desire is to be seen by everybody. They don't want to do anything in a private manner because they want to stand on street corners and use prayer benches so the world can understand this change is actually all about them and their unbelievably difficult life.

Watching some of them kneel down was an event in itself—as they walked slowly down the aisle and attempted to get down on their knees while avoiding flashing the congregation with some unsightly body part. In these moments you find yourself unable to look away, even though you know you should. Some people would not estimate the distance to the ground correctly, and end up slamming their knees into the carpet with a thud. Others went to the opposite side of the bench so they could look up to the heavens dramatically, quietly saying, "I'm ready for my close-up, Mr. DeMille." They each had their own style. One woman would fold her arms on the prayer bench in the shape of a parallelogram, place her head in the space provided, and begin crying, making sure her shoulders would shake so the congregation knew she was crying.

In fairness, I'm sure they all had real issues, and every now and then someone seemed sincere, but I watched it carefully because there wasn't much else to do and it was right in front of me. And I saw the pattern of behavior.

Those benches were our own little tiny wailing wall, used by the same five to ten church members every single Sunday.

Perhaps change should provide a wailing wall, or a punching bag, to let any people get out their fear and frustration. Maybe an emotional outlet would be a good way to keep things moving forward. But, for the most part, it is important to understand that some of your biggest obstacles will be people who will use the change process for attention. They will whisper doubt-creating questions to colleagues. They will suddenly have personal issues, complaints about their managers, and will need time off. And their negativity will suck the life out of everyone, robbing others of the energy needed for change.

Eventually, you take away expectations hoping the wailing will stop, but the prayer benches disproved that assumption. Even as the hymn died down, the sniffling of our afflicted would continue, and those of us in the congregation would begin the T.B. cough technique, often used by congregational members to try and end an uncomfortable moment (usually reserved for the unusually long periods of silent prayer).

Dad would look furtively to his left and right, hoping that the prayer-benchers would note the silence. But they reveled in it, this was their moment, and their sniffing would get louder and sometimes you could hear their "just" prayers...*just help me, Lord, just take my prayer and just help me*. The rest of us were praying that the Lord would just help them up so we could eat lunch.

Eventually, one or two would slowly rise with their backside to the church and their knees popping. Many in the congregation would smile supportively at them, while others would not make eye-contact, sure any reinforcement would delay lunch even further. But we knew that the next Sunday would bring the same people, because they had the bench. And they would milk it. One woman waited every single week until the **last** verse of the invitational hymn was being sung to work her way down the aisle with several seconds devoted to the process of kneeling. It took most of the verse to get her tears going. And she was the last to leave.

After several agonizing minutes, Dad would say something like "Well, we'll keep Dot in our prayers and give her some time to finish." Dot wouldn't move until somebody came up, put their hand on her shoulder and cried with her. We all dreaded Dot duty, but each one of us had to play the role at some point.

So, my issue with prayer benches isn't the location of them. It's that there are those who will use them for their own manipulation of others. And change requires positive association, not tears and fears. When implementing change, agents must be sure that they spotlight those who are trying, exhibiting courage, and making the new way work. While those who are lamenting should be heard, those who lament their one behavior should be seen as the manipulators that they are. This might sound cruel, but these people were religious exhibitionists who wanted attention, and we lost some good people because they were tired of the show.

Change is a delicate thing, and allowing people who are self-focused to cast a pallor on good effort cannot be allowed. This might mean quieting the retail leader who has only bad news at meetings, or ensuring that the most boring employee on the planet doesn't lead the most important sales meeting, especially when the honeymoon is almost over. Spotlight the right behavior, protect the positive and watch for displays of despair from the insincere.

CHANGE LESSONS

Encourage followers with signs of success.

Change starts with a pain point, but is kept alive by spotlighting what works. Why? Because everybody except your early adopters (who totally groove on anything different) are waiting for any reason to abandon ship. Change is exhausting because every new action requires conscious thought—nothing is "comfortable." Acknowledge those who are having success with the change, recognize them so that others can see those who are "going down the aisle" of your change. Positive energy gives people courage, while wailing pulls them back into their comfort zones. Propel people forward with small wins and acknowledge those wins throughout the company, especially when the change begins to escalate. Without this energy, you'll have early defectors.

Don't elevate the prayer bench people.

Some people love the drama of change, but for all the wrong reasons. They like the attention they can get when they complain about it, cry about it, moan and wail about it. You know the people. They sit in your meetings and say things like, "I think this is a great idea, but I don't know that my people can get this done because..." or "My department is so busy right now—we're exhausted and I have two women who have health issues as well as my own struggles that many of you know about..." I'm not saying there aren't legitimate concerns about change, and I'm not saying that all change is in the right direction. But when change is the right thing to do, and you hear these comments, you know they've come from a prayer bencher.

By the way, sometimes the prayer benchers will actually ask to be in positions of leadership during the change. They'll tell you how much they want to be a part of it, and you'll be tempted to give them a leadership role. Let them be a supporter, but don't let them be a leader. Their energy isn't going to become positive just because they have a new role. Any action they take will have one initiative...to get them more attention. And even if their motives are pure, their lack of positive energy will drag everybody down with them.

"Diseases always attack men when they are exposed to change."
–Herodotus

CHAPTER 12
WHEN IT'S TIME TO PREACH THAT SERMON

My dad's change strategy was never a generic strategy applied to any church, anywhere. There were always elements tailored to each church, their mission and their particular needs. He assessed the need by studying behavior and following his intuition. Many didn't know that Dad spent an hour in prayer every morning, treating it as a vision quest, a quiet time of meditation to get a sense of what the church and its members needed for that week. He tapped into that place that some call "soul," and asked his heart and gut to lead him through the Spirit who he served.

Once my parents had gathered energy, determined the disciples and created positive movement during the honeymoon phase, they knew it was time to buckle up for the bumpy ride of transition. It is said that everything is messy in the middle, which I resent as the middle child but also find to be basically true. My childhood pictures are filled with messy hair, cockeyed clothes and shoes with no socks. I was a mess.

Change is a lot like building a home. The blueprints are beautiful, and created sometimes before the decision to definitely build is confirmed. The plan is a dream on paper, with no financial debt or time delays tied to it. Then the decision is made, the builder determined, and the foundation poured. The framing happens quickly, and gives your dream a 3-D reality. The honeymoon is complete. Next comes the materials dumped that include Big Mac wrappers found and water puddling in your proposed living room. Wires are sticking out everywhere and the roof isn't on yet. If you visit the site during this period, you are sure it will never happen. Your dream is trashed. You yell at your contractor and consider selling the land and moving on. That's a lot like the transition phase of change. It's an emotional mess.

Dad prepared for this phase with a lot of meditation and prayer because he knew that at this stage everybody was going to wake up and smell the fear. And the brain will call for fight, flight or freeze, none of which are good options for a new leader. That's when Dad would ramp up information, provide Wednesday night conversations and begin to weave the changes through his sermons. We always led culture change, which is one of the most difficult types of changes. Research has shown that most culture change fails. We dealt with a big serving of culture that included religious belief. That mine field of belief made every move sensitive and exhausting for Dad, and because he was a Baptist minister he couldn't even drink.

The culture shift dad introduced involved building confidence and then moving towards a mission culture, one where the church serves others rather than entertaining itself with potlucks and non-threatening sermons. Dad and Mom wanted people to think, to be challenged, to take their faith seriously and never accept the simple answers provided by other ministers in much bigger churches. When people are afraid, they tend to feel like Indiana Jones running from that big rolling stone—sure it is aimed for them and not sure when it might stop rolling. Therefore, absolute clarity has to be a critical part of the call to change. People need to understand that things are going to get tough, and they need a clear roadmap. People seem to be willing to accept difficulty if they know it's coming. Therefore, Dad understood that he would have to literally announce the shift in intensity from the honeymoon phase to transition. Otherwise, he would surprise people. And as Daryl Conner (author of *Managing at the Speed of Change*) says:

"It's not the surprises in life that are so debilitating. The truly crushing force is being surprised that you are surprised."

My parents never tried to misrepresent this phase as a "big, fun, and exciting opportunity for growth." Much like someone entering an intense weight-loss program, the opportunity wouldn't be felt until those pounds start to come off, and those pounds don't come off until there is an absolute commitment to working hard and being uncomfortable for a while. Those who tiptoe around change, or try to use language that "spins" it into something fun, create greater fear through misrepresentation. Plus, when the truth comes out, trust is gone. Kind of like the time Dad told me that going on church visitations with him would be an exciting experience (because he needed a female to go with him and nobody else had shown up). I was still riding bikes and roller skating and jumping off swings. I knew exciting. Going to people's homes and listening to boring conversations with people who were nervous about having the minister in their home was in no way related to fun, not even a distant relative. From that point forward, I made Dad provide real-life job previews, so I could understand if I were actually going to get ice-cream or sit by the bed of someone on oxygen who didn't really know why I was there.

To eliminate surprise while announcing the need for courage and energy, Dad would deliver what we would affectionately call "that sermon." This would be the sermon that would boldly announce the mission, while touching on a core change issue. This would be the sermon that would cause a sea of smiling faces to suddenly look as if Kathy Bates were standing in front of the congregation with a board and sledgehammer.

"That sermon" fit the need of the current congregation, honed to an actionable mission statement. Dad's delivery directly addressed the particular issue that stood in the way of the church moving forward. The message might concern allowing women to serve, at which point he might preach a sermon about how Jesus was the greatest supporter of women in leadership roles. If the issue was monetary greed, he'd discuss a team in New England that began with the mission to save lives when ships were wrecked or lost at sea which turned slowly into a country club. When this happened, lives were lost while people spent more money on creating a nice country club environment that forgot to save people.

Take a moment, and think about how difficult it is to deliver a message that hits the heart of an uncomfortable truth, and do it in a way that would not cause a mass exodus that might shut down a cafeteria that was prepared to serve the early-arriving Presbyterians but would never be ready for an early group of Southern Baptists.

The night before "that sermon," Dad would let us know it was coming, which we kind of knew based upon the somber look on Mom's face as she reviewed his notes. But we were a team, and went into a quick denial using the energy to laugh our asses off because we knew that we were going to be sitting in hot water the next day.

The morning of "that sermon" included lots of gallows humor. We would debate if we should all dress in black and carry sickles, or simply provide the congregation with eggs and let them have at us during the altar call. Before arriving at the church, we generally had our own silent prayers, preparing for "that sermon" by putting on our spiritual armor. Most Sundays we would separate and sit with our friends, but on this day we stayed a unit, marching into church with smiling faces and the psychological weapon of optimism.

I remember one church in particular that struggled with reaching out to the poor. It's not that they didn't want to feed or clothe them, it's just that they didn't want them to actually show up in their sanctuary and depress them on Sunday morning. Dad's graduate work at Golden Gate Theological Seminary in San Francisco created the perfect sermon for this particular situation.

Because the class had been discussing mission work, the seminary professor brilliantly decided to help the ministers apply their knowledge. He told each of the ministers that they were going to be given one quarter and asked to live on the streets of San Francisco for three days as a homeless person. Each class member was told not to bathe or shave for a week, which was a treat, and caused us to empathize with the selfish church members who didn't want homeless people in their church.

I remember that Dad was really nervous about the potential dangers of this assignment, but anxious to understand what being homeless might feel like. The first morning of this three day trek he met with the professor, had his quarter tucked safely away, and hit the streets.

Dad was a terrible beggar. After two days he had bought one cup of coffee with his quarter and received less than a dollar in total contributions. He was now both homeless and starving, which began to build his true empathy for those who dealt with homelessness on a daily basis. He later talked about how uncomfortable he was approaching people, and was shocked by how many people refused to even look at him. He said a smile would have encouraged him, but the diverted eyes made him feel invisible. On one morning he stood hungry and exhausted outside of a church which had a service going on. He was sure that he had finally found a place where someone would offer to help him. He stood for 30 minutes, watching every single church member walk past him, talking about the great message they just heard without acknowledging the hungry man standing in front of them.

In a soup kitchen where volunteers made eye contact and offered food, Dad met other homeless people, and found them to be nothing like the stereotype of the lazy person that refuses to work for a living. One man had been a college professor when his wife and daughter were killed in a fire. He had simply lost the will to do anything. Another woman was bipolar, and didn't have access to the medical help she needed. He met teenagers that had run away from abusive homes and single mothers who were working three jobs but couldn't afford daycare and were afraid of losing their children to social services.

On his last night on the streets, Dad sat against a wall, defeated by hunger and a sense of hopelessness. Then he heard the voice of his Good Samaritan, "Sir, would you like to join me for dinner?" A sailor, recently disembarked from his ship, held a hand out to help dad off the ground. He introduced himself to Dad as if they were business colleagues, and didn't take him to the local McDonalds where he could purchase a to-go meal. Instead, that sailor took dad out to a steak dinner at a nice restaurant. Dad said a lot of eyes looked their way as he weaved through the tables smelling like someone who hadn't bathed in ten days and looking just as unappetizing. However, the sailor did not care because he acted as if they were best friends and they spent hours in conversation. The sailor didn't believe in God, but Dad said that young man provided the only Christian experience in his three days.

Dad finally completed his mission and came home, though much to our olfactory disgust, he maintained his homeless look until Sunday morning. We made him stand in the garage and/or backyard a lot that week. I think he used that alone time to get ready for the sermon that was going to put the angst in the change initiative.

Sunday morning finally arrived, and the sanctuary was filled with members anxious to see Dad in the pulpit again. Then there were those few financial rubberneckers that wanted proof that their money really went towards a seminary degree. For a variety of different reasons, the congregation was ready to have Dad back. Part of that enthusiasm came from weeks of listening to those that filled the pulpits

I always admired the courage of those deacons or church members that volunteered to preach, but listening to some of those sermons was similar to watching foreign film editors accepting their one and only Oscar. The sermons included lots of incoherent rambling in a language that, at least, seemed foreign, tied together with stumbling scripture and ending with awkward but sincere tears (and I mean from the congregation that was relieved it was finally over). People were ready for Dad.

That morning there was a buzz of energy, and everyone was in bright colors and quickly filled the front pews in the church, which in a Baptist church is a miracle in and of itself (hence the term "back-pew Baptists"). Suddenly, the choir walked in with equally big smiles. As the minister of music took his assigned spot to the right of the pulpit, everyone got quiet, as if a jury had just entered the courtroom with a verdict. You could see people straining to look around the person in front of them, hoping to get a glimpse of Dad as he returned from his doctoral program.

What they didn't realize was that Dad was already in their presence. He had quietly entered the sanctuary about five minutes earlier wearing dirty clothes, sporting a full beard, greasy hair, a baseball cap, sunglasses—and a lot of body odor. He walked about five pews in, and plopped down beside a nicely coiffed woman in her fifties who promptly stood up and left. She went out the back door, only to reemerge on the other side of the church within a few minutes sitting beside one of her friends.

Dad stood up, and moved up the aisle a few more pews. Those that noticed "the homeless man" immediately began to whisper as he passed by them. Who was this person? Was he going to be allowed to ruin the minister's first Sunday back? Dad became that guy on the bus that nobody wants sitting by them, and he watched some of his best church members frantically fill gaps in pews. He proceeded to sit down by a church family that had us over for dinner several times. Their five-year-old son seemed unfazed; he looked up, smiled at Dad and kept coloring his picture on the back of the bulletin. The parents, however, had a sudden need to scoot down the pew to the other end, giving lots of space between their confused little boy and the dirty man.

Dad smiled, and as he moved down the aisle, those that noticed him turned their heads and broke eye contact, lest he come their way. His final destination was the front pew, and he plopped down beside the deacons. Two deacons considered asking him to leave (much like Jesus would do ☺), but this is the moment when the minister of music walked in with the choir, and the whispers faded into silence.

Then it happened. The homeless man in the front pew slowly stood. The anticipatory smiles melted into disapproving frowns as he walked up the steps to the pulpit. He faced the choir briefly, and then turned to face the congregation.

Even as his child, I doubted that it was my father in front of that church. The homeless man stood at the pulpit, owning the space and pausing for several seconds so everyone could feel the discomfort. Then he lifted his right hand and smoothly removed his sunglasses. He put a hand on either side of the pulpit, leaned into the microphone, and uttered one simple word: "Hello."

The congregation let out a collective gasp that sucked back in all of the air created by previous whispers. Those who had moved in their pews when Dad sat behind them looked at their feet with red faces or looked around to see who they could blame for their gaff. The silence following the gasp felt so potentially explosive no one even dared to cough. "Hello." That one word was the emotional tripwire, and it could have been his entire sermon.

Dad knew that this church struggled with those who wanted it to be a mission church and those who wanted it to be a country club, so he told his story with no judgment. Using this approach let Dad tell a story that allowed the congregation to deduce the message they needed to hear without finger-pointing or blame. This sermon was important because it became the change catalyst for this church.

CHANGE LESSONS

Announce a shift in intensity.

Based upon what you've learned in your initial assessment, determine what the core issue is, and begin to chip away at it with a strong initial message upon which others will be built. If there is one thing people resist more than change itself, it's any change that surprises them. Therefore, leaders should announce their shift in intensity with the fact that behaviors and results must be dialed up because discomfort is a part of the deal. Change warriors don't have to be unpopular, but they probably will be for a while. Announcing a shift in intensity shows the commitment of leadership, because it says, "We're willing to be uncomfortable for a while to achieve this particular goal."

Provide "that message" in a way that touches the heart.

Stories allow audiences to derive the message needed without lectures that create defensiveness. In addition, stories touch a certain truth in the heart of people that reminds them of what's important. Dad could have lectured the country club crowd all day about how they treat people different from them and received only resistance; instead, he delivered a story that revealed the truth. Try remembering that people want to do the right thing, and sometimes a leader sharing a story humanizes the leader, and allows them to follow the integrity of coming to a conclusion without being commanded to go there.

"Loyalty to petrified opinions never yet broke a chain or freed a human soul." –Mark Twain

CHAPTER 13
MAKE THE CHANGE MISSION LIVE

Dad always knew that once the sermon had officially generated a stand, implementation of specific actions had to start immediately to show the change was there to stay. Not following "that sermon" with specific actions would leave people believing that this change would pass, that they could wait it out and the stand would be just another sermon. Too many business leaders have a brilliant kick-off where they verbally support the change and introduce the consultants involved. They fiercely state their commitment and sponsorship until the meeting is over. Then they wait for everybody else to implement the change while they go back to business as usual. We knew that action was the name of the game, and when it was announced, there was no option to take a step back into normalcy.

When mission work was the chosen stand, Dad would quickly select a few members of the community that could benefit from a partnership so that he could quickly enroll church members in contributing through action. He knew that people believed what they saw, and they had to see that he was taking action. So he would engage key disciples to help find a community mission or church. He knew that influence wasn't found in someone else's experience, but in the collective experience found in taking action. Perhaps this was a reason missionary slides never resulted in someone else deciding to become a missionary. If done, I'm pretty sure research would show that excessive hours spent viewing mission slides can result in a form of PTSD. Okay, that's a slight exaggeration, but to this day I have nightmares that include badly dressed missionaries standing in front of generic foliage, boring to death those to whom they were ministering. I still flinch if I hear the ka-cha, ka-cha, ka-cha sound of slides changing in the projector.

Mom and Dad made sure that our mission projects were more personal than watching slides. In some churches, we partnered with "sister" Hispanic churches that were in low-income areas. In others, we opened coffee shops in high-crime areas or held Friday night youth programs to attract kids in tough home situations. We didn't just beat people over the heads with our Bibles or beliefs. Instead we actually helped them. It's funny how helping to fix someone's house has more power than walking into their broken-down homes and telling them how they should worship God.

Lecturing people about something rarely results in changed behavior, mostly because people are waiting for the lecture to end so they can go back to what they were doing. And leaders who have no intention of getting scared and grimy by entering the arena of change offer empty words, and often include empty emails. Their words mean nothing to those who know they aren't doing a thing different. Dad made us put our mission work into action. This included the youth group offering their Saturdays to do yard work for people who needed it most.

I'll never forget one older lady whose husband had died, leaving her financially destitute. Dad found out about her situation through a neighbor that was a church member, and they had let her know a few of the church's youth group members would be coming to help her one Saturday afternoon. We pulled up in four cars to a small, white clapboard house that was so overrun by brush and weeds that you barely noticed the house itself. We saw large piles of wood climbing precariously up the right side of the house, a white picket fencing exhibiting a sad smile with several teeth missing and wildflowers peeking around high weeds.

We stepped out of our cars tentatively and followed a brick path where most of the bricks had sunk beneath the dirt under the weight of past friends and family. We approached the front door with black paint cracked and peeling, on which a screen door hung jauntily cock-eyed. We knocked on the door and waited for several minutes while bugs buzzed us and the elderly neighbor next door stood guard in her side window, peering through the wide aluminum blinds.

We wondered if we had the wrong address, or if we had wandered up to an abandoned house. Then we heard the doorknob jiggling, and the door opened slowly as if a ghost were the inhabitant. Then we saw her—a little woman with gray hair, with an old, ripped house dress and a beatific smile that made every dingy thing around us disappear. I will call her Mrs. Anderson.

"Oh, you came. Thank you, thank you, thank you!" Her chin began to quiver, and tears started to run down her cheeks. We were just teenagers, so we looked at each other awkwardly, unaware of how to handle immediate emotion. Luckily our youth minister smiled and said, "You are more than welcome, Mrs. Anderson. We're glad we could come today. Why don't you show us around your yard and we'll decide what to do first?" Mrs. Anderson's feet swelled over the tops of her black shoes, and she wobbled in obvious pain. She pointed to the backyard, and since we could barely see anything other than over-grown bushes, weeds and the stacked wood sure to be filled with black widow spiders, we had an idea of where we needed to start. We walked Mrs. Anderson back inside so she could sit down and put her feet up.

We put on our gloves, sprayed ourselves with bug spray and got to work. Our morning hours were spent re-stacking wood that she could use, clearing weeds and throwing away fifteen years' worth of collected trash. Under the weeds, we found a nice brick patio, lovely stone steps, and some determined flowers that reflected a happy past. While the discoveries were interesting, the work was exhausting, espe-cially for teenagers who spent a lot more time sitting than working.

Two hours into raking, digging, and filling trash bags in the heat, we heard the back patio sliding glass door open. We turned to see Mrs. Anderson wobbling across the newly uncovered brick patio. In her slightly shaking hands was an old metal serving tray with ten stale cookies, a couple of half sandwiches, and a pitcher of weak lemonade. Our youth minister ran to her and took the tray, placing it on an old picnic table. She clapped her hands together and said, "You all are just working so hard, I thought you could use a snack." Her smile lit up the backyard, and we choked back tears as we realized she was probably offering us the little bit of food she had in her own pantry. "I wish it could be more," she said, her voice cracking. "And I want you to know my husband and I kept this house neat as a pin when he was alive. It wasn't always like this." We all let her know it was more than enough, and because of the immense effort and sacrifice of her contribution, it was.

Our group worked non-stop on her yard the rest of the day, our spirits boosted by the fresh gratitude expressed by the stale cookies. The front and backyard looked transformed. Like an Etch-a-Sketch, we had shaken away the brambles and weeds to reveal a charming little house that still delivered on personality alone. We had painted shutters, swept sidewalks, placed flowers on her porch and uncovered so many beautiful examples of a home well-loved. When we showed Mrs. Anderson our handiwork, she grasped our hands and gasped with delight. "Well, there is our brick patio. I knew it was still there—my husband and I spent months building that together." She proceeded to weave stories about all of the small delights we had uncovered while tears of joy and memory streamed down her face.

We spent one day with Mrs. Anderson, but she gave us a lifetime of lessons with her simple joy and sincere gratitude. Remember, we were a bunch of teenagers more aware of the opposite sex than little old ladies, but Mrs. Anderson changed our perception. We were all so touched by the experience, we wanted to share it with the entire church. It sounds so corny to say, "She gave us more than we ever gave her," but it's absolutely true. To this day, I can see her carrying that tray, I can see her tears, and I can feel the warmth of her smile. Dad knew what would happen if he let us truly experience the beauty and breadth of missions, so he let us share the story with the rest of the church. Dad knew that we would find in Mrs. Anderson more than a day's worth of work. Through our efforts at her house, we would find the passion to change.

It's critical that leaders tie change to emotions, and make sure they understand the "why" of it all. When people realize the value in something and understand how it is going to impact them, they'll work their fingers to the bone to make it happen. But had we just lectured Mrs. Anderson on our mission, and how special we were, and then left without touching her yard, nothing would have been accomplished.

Unlike a sermon, or slides, Dad understood that when we shared our story about that day we gave the change initiative a face; no longer was this just another task that made people uncomfortable. Now it was the face of a beautiful woman with a loving past who shared the last of her cookies and lemonade with those who helped her. This one woman made change disciples of many of us in that church.

CHANGE LESSONS

This too shall NOT pass.

Once "that sermon" has been delivered, the energy created by the message must be used to propel specific actions forward. People have to know the change is going to stick, and that there is a good reason why. Something has to make them feel a part of the change, and touch the heart. Trying to remove emotion from change is like cutting the heart out of the body and then wondering why it's dying. The center of every organization is the heartbeat of those in it. Any leader who does not believe that will run things well for a while, but there will be no passion and no sense of purpose. That's how sweatshops are created, and they destroy those who work within their walls. A great change leader wants a group of people who are awake and energized, so they offer immediate action that enrolls those who are recipients of that change. The fact that people are given specific ways to start moving forward is important for establishing direction and immediate momentum. If you miss the chance to build on "that sermon," the message will have to be delivered again and will break the trust of those impacted.

Give the change initiative a face.

It took one face, moved from tears to joy, to truly kick the change effort into practice. Whether you're changing systems or culture, there has to be a human element that shows those who will be driving the change are a critical part of the process. Dad could have had the best sermon in the world about Mrs. Anderson, but having us see the value of our work and the change in her saved a year of sermons to motivate the heart. And having the disciples share their story showed engagement by those already living the commitment. You can have the greatest process in the world, but if you don't motivate the hearts of the people that have to make the process work, you'll lose the change effort before it even gets started. Combine momentum with a sense of purpose, and the change will be propelled forward.

It takes tremendous courage to change, and when people can serve others and play an important part in the change, they develop a sense of purpose that can get them through the tough times.

> "It is uncertainty that creates the space for invention. We must let go, clear the space, leap into the void of not knowing, if we want to discover anything new." –Margaret Wheatley

CHAPTER 14

WHEN THE WORST SINGERS WANT SOLOS

N
ow that change in the church was in full swing and the mission was living and breathing through specific heart-engaging actions, it was time for my parents to enroll some of the more hesitant. My parents always knew that once change was really starting to happen, they needed to get as many people on board as possible because they'd statistically lose a considerable amount of the church members once things started to get tough. Without any fancy change theories, my family figured out that there was a direct correlation between the level of change difficulty and the number of followers that stayed with us during these periods:

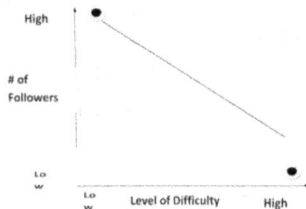

We found that most people in the church broke into three key categorical types:

The Shrews: One of the smallest mammals on earth, the shrew is fiercely territorial, and will drive off rivals much bigger than themselves. My family consistently found that 20% of the church congregation would be the opinion leaders who declared their territories and dug in their heels for the upcoming battle. In our experience, about 10% of the shrews were in favor of the change, and about 10% were against changing anything. What we later realized is that those members tend to be the Hatfields and McCoys, Bears and Packers, Jets and Sharks of the church, consistently taking opposite sides on every issue. They really weren't battling change as much as they were battling each other. Regardless, they were the opinion leaders and became either our greatest supporter or biggest gut buster.

The Rabbits: Rabbits have a great deal of energy, but they tend to hop around with no general sense of destination. We found that this group made up about 30% of the church congregation. They loved positive energy and hopped around pews visiting folks before and after services. However, as change became more difficult, they seemed to get disoriented and tended to hop to the next "happy" church. They didn't tolerate hard work very well, and appeared to think that any environment not filled with large crowds and lots of hallelujahs were emitting some kind of poison that would "bring them down."

While it's not that we didn't want rabbits in our church (they were great energizers when times were good) we found that we couldn't count on them to stick it out through the tough times. About 10% of the rabbits would hop the Sunday after "that sermon." The rest would arrive with big eyes and fluffy tails for about a month and their ears drooping with every challenge until they hopped away. Interestingly enough, we found that once things were positive again, about half of the rabbits hopped back into the sanctuary since they were now disenchanted with their new environment. We couldn't depend on them, but we did appreciate them when they were around.

The Turtles: The turtles' shells developed from their ribs over millions of years to act as a shield to protect their soft bodies. My family found that there are church members who seem to act in a similar fashion. These church members were happy when everybody else was happy, but emotional shells were quickly formed when the going got tough. They believed church as the one place where they wouldn't need protection, so they often retreated when the conversations turned to more heated debates. Business meetings on Wednesday nights often involved the most cost-conscious of the congregation to bellow about our heating bill, at which point another member would stand up to defend the family as it was the middle of winter. Dad would finally intervene and agree to some compromise, but by that time the turtles were in their shells and shut down.

They made up about 50% of the church, and while their tenacity prevented them from actually leaving the church physically, they would tend to simply pick their side in the shrew category and sit quietly with their supporters. They just wanted peace, so they formed their shells, pulled in their heads and let the Shrews battle it out. Often we would find they would only attend one or two Sundays a month during the toughest part of the change, when congregants were lashing out due to their fear of transition, but they reemerged once the storm had passed.

Every organization has those shrews who tend to survive every leader, either as adaptive supporters or as those who refuse to leave their place of work for any reason but fight for control. They are neither good nor bad, but there needs to be an awareness of them to understand how difficult the change effort would be. The Rabbits are also present in organizations, jumping to another place where a friend was housed or an old boss had landed, just avoiding the pressure. And the Turtles brought the same lunch in the same Tupperware dish, and sat in meetings saying as little as possible.

Dad was always very sensitive to the Rabbits and the Turtles because he understood their reluctance and concerns about the challenge to their routines and increased conflict as new ideas were implemented. For example, when dad asked that for one Sunday night a quarter we visit our "sister" Hispanic church. Dad would preach there, and the congregation was invited, but few actually showed up. His hope was to build a bridge between the cultures, but the Rabbits and Turtles loved their routine and weren't comfortable with the switch. He knew that he had to enroll as many of them as powerfully as possible, so that they would be more likely to stay with the church. Every now and then I would watch a Rabbit or Turtle become stronger, more resilient and willing to take a stand for change. Some began visiting the Hispanic church, and became passionate about the mission opportunities as the two ministers formed a commitment to serve each other. Because they weren't contentious by nature, their comments in business meetings held more weight than those of the shrews (of whom everybody expected a fight).

Dad used several key strategies to strengthen the Turtles and try to keep the Rabbits from hopping away too quickly. First of all, he would build up their confidence by making them part of a key initiative—most often the church service. My mom was often frustrated by this part of the change because she loved liturgical, beautiful services with great soloists and moving prayers, and that desire was getting ready to face the meteor of the unconsciously incompetent. Dad's attempt to enroll lay people in the service meant that sometimes the most awkward speakers would want to pray in front of the church, and the tone-deaf would suddenly feel led to not only join the choir but to have a solo.

While my family knew that inclusion was the best strategy to enroll undecided members, we would hope with each church that those with the greatest talent would step forward. Alas, they were generally not nearly as interested as Beatrice who sang bass in choir and had such a low range she should have come with sub-woofers, or Larry who sang so quietly only dogs could hear him and would accompany himself with a badly played electric guitar. We knew that we could only use the excuse "the service is already planned, which is a shame because we'd love to have you be a part" so many times or we'd have another disgruntled congregational member on our hands.

Therefore, one Sunday night a month (yes, always on a Sunday night), those in search of a tune would get to share their gift while the rest of us kept repeating silently, "God thinks this is beautiful, God thinks this is beautiful." Looking back now, I believe God must have found the off-key attempts courageous, but beautiful was a stretch.

While our ears were assaulted by such uplifting tunes as "Why Me, Lord" (a title we always felt should have been dedicated to the listeners), the solos were broken up only by the awkward prayers of the earnest. I know that it is surely some kind of sacrilege to make fun of someone's prayer, but people need to have a firm grasp of what they should never do in public. Even I, as a preacher's kid, knew that praying was not my forte. I was too conscious of my word choice, and I couldn't really think of any appropriate messages. For those of you who did not grow up Southern Baptists, we rarely have recitation type prayers (other than the "Lord's Prayer," where we still stumble over the choice between Trespassers and Debtors). Baptists always do it the hard way—full immersion rather than sprinkling, and original prayers rather than memorized. I was always envious of my friends that could recite prayers and creeds all day long without being forced to think of something original over and over again.

I was asked once to lead a closing prayer in Sunday School by the teacher who seemed to think it was my duty since I was the daughter of the minister. I politely declined with a firm, "no thank you." I wasn't going to punish other church members by stumbling through a self-conscious message to God. To me, praying publicly was like yelling out something that should only be whispered into your best friend's ear. And I wasn't going to be like some of those associate ministers who used their prayer time to elicit a small sermon since they didn't get to preach as often as they'd like.

While enrollment of people is important during times of change, it's also important to understand their skills and ensure those talents are appropriately put to use. Remember, change is a delicate thing. Perhaps a CEO planned a town hall meeting to provide an enthusiastic update, but an introvert's stumbling through the notes on a poorly constructed slide turned it into a disaster.

There is a chance of engaging some people at the demotivation of the many. So, what do you do?

You pay careful attention to each situation, and sometimes you use your intuition. Despite the downside, we knew that the cost of ostracizing possible supporters was greater than our desire for quality solos or prayers. We didn't always have to accept every person's voluntary contribution, but sometimes we felt it was smarter to sacrifice presentation to add a little heart. If the request was heartfelt, then we went with it. That solo often meant the world to the person singing it and that awkward prayer was often shared by someone who was facing a real change in their life who wanted to express it. Most importantly, the more involved people were in change, the more they supported it. Once enrolled, they were no longer being commanded to change because they became an organic part of it. As a result, this propelled it forward because they mattered.

Others, even the crazy talented, who wanted only a platform for their own glory, could be more damaging. Their lack of passion and desire for applause would supersede their devotion, and Dad could sniff that out very quickly. So, we had some bad solos and some awkward prayers, but we also felt the accelerated beating of the heart of change in those moments as more people yearned to be involved.

CHANGE LESSONS

Know your followers and be prepared for fallout.

Understand that the way people react to change is the same whether you are leading a church or a corporation. As a change warrior, you will be faced with the tenaciously loyal Shrews and the Rabbits who are ready to hop to a department not facing change. This has consequences because the Turtles that lose their energy will retreat into their shell and offer little to no assistance. Understand that your job is knowing which category your people fall into, and determining how you might be able to motivate Turtles and Rabbits and focus the Shrews. At the end of the day, people want to do what is right. The question is whether it is right for them, or for the overall mission.

Intuitively determine your most passionate people.

Many of your most important employees are not in touch with their true talent and want to be involved in ways that do not use their best skills. Make an attempt to help people contribute where their skill lies if possible. If you have someone who fancies themselves a motivational speaker but is actually much more fluent in organization, have them organize the project and allow them to give updates as their motivational speaking opportunity. More importantly, gauge their passion. If they truly feel led to share a message or be part of a committee and are enthusiastic about the change, then the charge they provide the heart of the organization could be enough because sincerity always wins over salesmanship. For those who want to be part of something for attention, it gives them that at the highest level. They are the very team members who will undermine the effort if it shines a less than brilliant light on them. Desire and passion trump talent, but the best of all results is to match skills with positions that will help drive the change. Have someone with experience join a novice group to provide wisdom from past decisions; have a hot project manager be put in charge of helping organization tactical steps; have a person with a passion for strategy provide feedback on the change vision. Rotate people in and out of positions to keep the energy high and help focus your Shrews on positively leading the effort. To add on, give accolades to the quiet team members who make a big difference. And every now and then, give an assignment to someone who makes up in enthusiasm what is lacking in slick talent. Sometimes their heart is exactly what the change needs.

"Life is, for most of us, a continuous process of getting used to things we hadn't expected." –Martha Lupton

CHAPTER 15
WHEN RETIRED PEOPLE KILL YOUR DISHWASHER

e can fix it at no cost, so there is no need to call a professional. These kind words uttered by well-meaning retired people in the congregation can be the kiss of death for your house, car or yard. Their hearts are in the right place, but their abilities rarely match their desire to save the church some money and get to wear a tool belt at the same time. This fact, along with a lack of urgency and some rubber band fixes, elongated our parsonage problems.

There would be extra cost involved once multiple repairmen tried to fix what the retirees broke with their good intentions. And they would show up in a few days while water flooded the house or we froze without heat. I think the assumption was that since they weren't charging us anything, we should be grateful. On the other hand, we needed a greater sense of urgency and were actually willing to pay to get it. But it wasn't our house.

Change is like this—it can't be driven by complacency or efficiency. I've witnessed many companies that made plenty of money and simply weren't in enough pain to move quickly. They liked to play with new ideas, and talk about things like innovation and being a thought-leader, but they didn't have a dire need to be either. They brought in so much money just being them that they decided talking about change was enough. The problem was, they weren't preparing for the future. They were just sitting like satiated kings of the industry in the present. Change requires a certain level of pain, because pain is what drives urgency.

For example, when I was 16 years-old, my parents went to Sussex, England, on a mission trip. My siblings and I were left with the parsonage, and our goal was to have the house clean for their return. In addition, after some church members witnessed my 115 lb. mother trying to push the old dishwasher that connected to the sink with a hose back into the kitchen after dinner, they surprised us with a built-in dishwasher. Along with that, two retirees had volunteered to install it several months earlier.

Our goal was to get that big box out of the middle of our tiny kitchen and have it installed before Mom and Dad returned from England. Our volunteers had shown up the day before, and installed it for us. They were over a month late, probably very busy fixing a lot of things they had previously broken, but we were grateful. The night before my parent's return, however, it started to leak. Surprisingly, the dishwasher installed by an ex-banker and an ex-insurance salesman was not working. We called the minister of music, who promised our volunteers would be out first thing in the morning. I asked if we could just call someone who actually worked on dishwashers, but was told I should let them fix their own work. It was free, after all.

On the day my parents were to return I woke up early, blew dry my Farah Fawcett hair (the only era where my frizzy, thick hair had a real purpose) and got ready to go to school. As I walked downstairs to get breakfast, I heard voices (another downside to a parsonage—people tend to let themselves in without knocking). I heard a lot of banging, and then I started to make out their words:

"Charlie—can you see where the leak is coming from?"

"Nope, can't see a thing under here. I need to get my glasses. Maybe if I pull this..."

"Slow it down, Charlie—now the water is really flowing. What did you pull?"

"That hose right there. I guess I shouldn't have done that..."

I walked slowly down the stairs as if entering a Freddy Krueger nightmare. Every step brought with it a sense of greater dread. As I got to the bottom of the stairs, I saw water leaking beyond the kitchen onto our hardwood floors in the dining room. I gritted my teeth, feeling my teenager rage starting in my toes and working its way to my mouth. As I sloshed into the kitchen, I saw a small but not lovely fountain that was spewing water out from under the dishwasher. Water now covered the tops of my feet, and I stared at the two volunteers with an anger I still cannot describe. All the years of having people without skill working on our parsonage when we were willing to pay some-body else to do the work, came spilling out. We'd had more things broken and then awkwardly put things together than I could count and we always had to act grateful. *Not today* I told myself, and I grabbed my hair with my hands like a crazy woman, and yelled out:

"What the hell are you doing? What is all this shit?"

Yes, the preacher's daughter was spewing forth obscenities like the proverbial sailor. In self-defense, I was aware that neither one of these men had ever held a job that even remotely prepared them to fix anything. They were both white-collar professionals that apparently felt blue overalls and a new tool belt made them handy. Regardless, I shouldn't have been so ungrateful and rude. My youth only saw old people messing up the kitchen on a day I wanted to impress my parents. As I am now the age of the guys doing the fixing, I find them much more noble. I should have said "Wow, thanks for showing up three months late and the day before my parents are coming home and volunteering when you have no idea what you're doing thus preventing us from getting real help." Okay, so I'm still bitter.

Creating urgency in people who have no skin in the game is impos-sible. You can't entice people to successfully embrace change if they don't have a real reason to change in the first place. It's like fire drills at school—nobody moves quickly and quietly out the door. Half of the students linger in hallways talking to friends. Why? Because there is no fire. Change is the same way. Take away the catalyst to get it moving and there is no way to propel people faster. These two volun-teers were wealthy, relaxed and had no idea how much a new dish-washer meant to us.

But cursing at people and trying to make them feel your pain doesn't work either. Once the words were out of my mouth, I tried to quickly recover with some charming chit-chat, but it didn't work. They turned off the water and left the house because I think they didn't know what to do to fix it, but I can't prove it. My parents came home to lots of wet towels, a defensive teenager and a house with no water. Within thirty minutes of them entering the home, they received a cool call from one of the wives about my abhorrent behavior.

I had to personally apologize to each of the men and Dad had to deal with lots of conversations about a daughter with a temper and foul mouth to match. I had offended volunteers that were offering time at no cost, and I had revealed a flaw in the family of the change warrior at the same time, something the cheek-kissers could quickly escalate. And that made it a tough lesson learned. What was assumed to be the ultimate benefit of saving money had ceased to have any appeal for us after several months of skirting around a huge box in the middle of a tiny kitchen. We would have taken out a loan to pay someone to install the dishwasher, but we weren't allowed to do that since the church owned the house. And therein lies another change truth—when people feel they have no control over a situation and are never asked for input, you can misinterpret what is important to them. That's where the disciples are critical because they keep their finger on the pulse of the real pushback and not what shows up in meetings.

In my situation, I should have simply smiled, thanked them for trying, and let them turn the water off. I could have still cleaned up the water, dusted, vacuumed and welcomed my parents with a smile. Instead, I gave those opposed to change a platform upon which they would stand for months to come. Worst of all, I made the good guys mad.

CHANGE LESSONS

When dealing with pressure, hold your tongue.

The second phase of change can be filled with pressure, and it's the smallest word or event that might crush the spirit or flare the temper. Remember that every message, particularly from the change warrior, is magnified when change is escalating. Every event is hyper-analyzed and judged with greater intensity (and sometimes less fairly). The resulting drama could damage the change effort and people who have volunteered to help might not have the same level of urgency as the change warrior themselves. Perhaps they came in late to the conversation, or aren't even sure what all the fuss is about. What is a benefit to them might not match what is an actual benefit to the leader of change. They might want to save the company money when the change has to do with growth. Efficiency never grew anything.

No matter how great your frustration is during times of change, as the agent you must hold your tongue. A few simple words said in anger can be held up for everyone to see as evidence of the disaster coming called "change." I learned my lesson the hard way.

A flaw in leadership can fuel resistors.

If a change warrior shows a weakness too early in the process, followers begin to question the intelligence of their own loyalty to the change. No one wants to be wrong about who they support, especially if the change is starting to show levels of difficulty. But when a leader shows fear or appears upset or nervous, the followers are going to stop following. Remember, this is when rabbits and turtles start to disappear. A flaw shown prematurely can undo months of confidence building. Even worse, that flaw becomes something resistors will grasp and use to beat down the effectiveness of the change warrior.

"Alas! How enthusiasm decreases, as our experience increases!"
–Louise Colet

CHAPTER 16

DRIVING A TAXI THAT SAYS "JESUS SAVES"

Tony owned a taxi cab company in a very tough area in California, and had little patience for "touchy-feely" things like faith. While his wife attended our church, he was a self-proclaimed angry atheist. Tony stood about 6'3" and weighed over 300 lbs. He had dark hair, sleeve tattoos (which weren't as common as they are today), and a constant scowl on his face. Let's just say you wouldn't be surprised if you saw Tony on a *Law & Order* episode as the rough dock worker who refuses to testify against the bad guy.

As always, Dad's purpose was simply to connect with him at first, not convert him, and so he stayed in conversation with Tony. When Dad visited per his wife's request, they didn't talk about faith unless Tony wanted to. Instead, Dad asked him about his business and showed a sincere respect for what Tony did for a living. My grandfather owned a small construction company and Dad's first job was as a bricklayer, so Dad respected hard work and business sense. Tony's ice cold exterior slowly thawed as he realized Dad was not judging him. One year later, this tough atheist became a part of the church and a major player in the change arena. His enthusiasm and energy were raw but offered a bright light that helped illuminate hope in a tough year that had the potential to wipe my parent's enthusiasm out completely.

Change is like that; it can convert the most unexpected individuals. Those who are often the most adamantly opposed to the change suddenly make a turn. The person who voiced the most objections in every meeting has an epiphany of sorts, realizing that change is not there to hurt but to help. They are often people who don't play games, say what everyone else is thinking, and inadvertently surface fears for the group. Once you accomplish getting these people on board, their enthusiasm is unrelenting in the best of ways.

One day, Tony told Dad that he had a big surprise for the church that he would reveal at the conclusion of the next Wednesday night service. He mentioned that we would need to gather in the parking lot to see his gift. So, following our next Wednesday night service, those of us who didn't feel a need to run home lest they get recruited into choir or visitation, quickly gathered in the parking lot at the back of the church. A dark evening in this neighborhood often involved the sounds of sirens, so we all stood a little nervously, checking over our shoulders. Suddenly, Tony appeared around the corner lighting up that dark parking lot with a smile that illuminated everything around him. Tony said, "What I am getting ready to give to this church is because of Pastor Joe, and because he believed in me when I didn't. Stand still, I'll be right back." We all looked at each other, but stayed incredibly quiet. Against the backdrop of anticipation, we heard the sound of a car engine.

My dad looked at all of us with a smile that registered both delight and a sense of dread. It was one thing to bring Tony into the church fold, but it was another to accept a gift that may or may not be acceptable to the congregation. So, we all waited quietly as the engine sound grew louder and louder. Around the corner of the church came a light, not the light of an angel, but the headlights of an old taxi-cab that had been painted red, white and blue. On top of the cab, replacing the light that usually says "Taxi-Cab," was Tony's extra special surprise. The light now said "Jesus Saves."

I watched Dad's face as the gift registered, and he looked like a proud papa that was wondering how to proudly display a tacky Father's Day gift. Tony stepped out from behind the wheel with a huge smile, and that big tough man broke into tears as he presented the keys to Dad. He said that he figured Dad needed an official car to make home visitations, and he was presenting this taxi in honor of Dad's visitations that ultimately resulted in his relationship with the church.

I think Dad got teary-eyed as well, both out of his affection for Tony and because he would now have to drive this taxi-cab to people's homes for visitation. I'm sure he envisioned hundreds of doors being slammed before he could even say hello. My poor father, who believed in the power of faith but avoided the pull of propaganda, now had to drive the "Jesus Saves" mobile.

It is rarely the shiny corporate person who creates passion from the middle out. Instead, it is one employee who realizes that change could make their life better. This is the employee who throws all of his objections at the change warrior to see what will stick. This is your courageous follower who becomes an informal leader who puts incredible energy into their pushback until they feel the urge to pull right along with leadership.

While we all stood applauding and choking down our laughter, Dad took his place behind the wheel. He invited Tony to join him as a passenger. As they drove away for a test drive, Dad turned to us, smiled and tooted the horn. Because he was a man of integrity, my dad spent the next year of visitation nights driving his "Jesus Saves" cab, and our big tough Tony remained absolutely committed to his new faith and the change effort. His gift helped keep people in the church moving forward, keeping us focused on giving to each other rather than creating new, petty arguments. People in the tough neighborhood around our church soon learned that "Pastor Joe" drove the Jesus-Saves-Mobile. As he would drive down the street on Monday nights, he would honk and they would wave. Somehow, that crazy cab brought the whole neighborhood together.

CHANGE LESSONS

Enthusiasm is expressed through the filter of individual personality.

When asking for enthusiasm, remember that you can't always control how enthusiasm will be expressed. People might energize their own workspace with unapproved decor, or inspired managers may park a popcorn machine somewhere they shouldn't to keep energy high. While corporate regulation might mean you have to control some forms of enthusiasm, remember that when change gets tough, there is nothing that renews energy like the power of someone who has a fresh heart. They come on board when the change warriors are tired, when the early adopters have lost some energy and the party-poopers are gaining speed.

As change gets tough, you might find hope in the least likely personalities.

Sometimes those agreeable sorts that are SO excited about the change when you're presenting it actually turn off the light of enthusiasm as soon as you walk out the door. Others that seem a little more prickly and resistant often become your change oasis. Look for potential supporters by watching for specific actions, including the expression of objections. Any voiced objection shows a person is putting energy into consideration of the change. Don't be mesmerized by words of support; instead, be enchanted by actions that move the change forward. Hope, during times of change, can be found in the least likely of places.

"Our deeds determine us, as much as we determine our deeds."
–George Eliot

CHAPTER 17

NERVOUS LAUGHTER AND FALSE TEETH

Once change warriors enroll more followers in preparation for the critical second phase of the change process, they have to be ready to deal with any obstacle that comes their way. If phase one is the honeymoon, phase two ends up being an emotional obstacle course that would challenge the most mentally athletic of us.

I remember one church, in particular, that was beautiful, but the neighborhood around it had slowly become a high-crime area. Within this neighborhood was a charming slumlord (yes, I'm being snide) who ran a series of apartment buildings which housed mentally ill people released from psychiatric centers due to lack of funding. Those people ended up being some of our favorite church members—particularly James.

James used to shuffle into church each Sunday, dressed in his one dirty pair of khakis, an old yellowed dress shirt and a tweed jacket that housed more holes than tweed. I remember his gait because he walked a lot like a pigeon with his head leading the way in a bouncing rhythm. His red face was topped with thinning, strawberry blond hair and he stood about 5' 7". Every time he entered the sanctuary, he would stop in the doorway and take off his hat with respect, holding it with both hands as if it would protect him from the stares. Oh, and one more thing, James had a nervous laugh that never stopped. As his head rocked forward, the laugh would increase in volume and as it rocked back, it would get softer. What made it unique was the laughing never stopped.

I found James a little pathetic at first, and then extremely annoying. His behavior was disruptive to my dad's sermons, and I was protective of him. What we didn't know at first but later discovered was that James had been hit by a train as an adolescent and suffered brain damage. That damage caused him to laugh uncontrollably, but as a fourteen-year-old, I just knew it wasn't good when a minister was trying to make an emphatic point about someone's spiritual life while someone is laughing like the minister is Jerry Seinfeld delivering some of his best material. Before we got used to James, all of us would watch with dread as he picked his pew for the day.

Although James rarely spoke, he always nodded at people respect-fully by kindly tipping his hat to the ladies. He took his faith seriously, and even though he laughed through most sermons, he listened to every word. In fact, James took one of Dad's sermons to heart quickly and took action on the message. Dad had spoken about the widow who gave the only thing she owned of value to Jesus—her two small coins. While Dad had been figuratively referencing giving your time and heart to God, James took it literally and realized all he had of any value were his false teeth.

Every Sunday from that point forward James would bow his head as he held the offering plate, remove his false teeth and place them gently among the envelopes and cash. This offered a ghoulish display for the rest of the congregation who had yet to give their money. The plate, like James, looked as if it were laughing.

While James's heart was in the right place, the deacons had the unfortunate task of giving James his teeth back at the end of each Sunday service. The returner was generally determined by flipping a coin in the foyer, and the loser would grab a paper towel, pick up the unlikely offering and return them to James. He would always graciously accept them back with a smile, popping them back in so that they could continue to be a partner in his laughter. In his heart, he had given to God something precious, even if it was only for a few minutes.

James had listened intently to the message, which resulted in his giving what little he had to offer. Change requires people and leaders to listen closely to what is being shared. Because in an environment where the very foundation of comfort is shifting, emotions will run high and decisions could be impulsive. James heard what Dad had to say, and he responded in a way that was appropriate for him. Sometimes, we need to stop worrying about having the perfect teammates and value what they bring to the table. James was at church every Sunday. He listened, gave what he could give and he had a talent nobody knew about.

Dad had an incredible way of paying attention to everyone. He spent time with James while the rest of us nervously avoided him and worried about how many more James-like characters the Sunday service could handle. Since James only communicated through laughter, Dad did most of the talking. It was quite a sight, seeing Dad behind his desk talking while James sat across from him, hat in his lap, rocking back and forth, laughing. I'll never forget the Sunday that James walked down that aisle to join the church. He laughed louder than usual—can you imagine the strength it took for him to take that walk? Dad greeted him like a long-lost brother, and even the most judgmental of us had tears in our eyes. Dad knew that people like James were the ones Jesus referenced when he said, "Feed my sheep." And he knew James had something amazing in his heart, hidden by the physical and mental damage inflicted by the train.

One weeknight, Dad was in his study, thinking that he was alone. Suddenly he heard hymns being played on a piano with such classical flare he was sure the minister of music had come in and was listening to tapes. Dad walked out of his office, calling the minister of music's name. Nobody responded. Dad followed the sound of the music. He opened the swinging door to the sanctuary and realized someone was actually playing "Amazing Grace" on the church piano. Now he was intrigued, and he took a few more steps to see who the talented musician might be. The rocking motion gave him away instantly.

Dad stood, listening, moved beyond words. He said James had the touch of a classical pianist and that he didn't laugh at all when he played. As Dad stood there, James realized he was no longer alone, so he stopped playing and began to laugh nervously again. Dad realized that James wanted no audience, so he simply said, "James, I'll stay in my office. But any night that I'm here alone, you can play as long as you'd like." While James's expression rarely changed, Dad said he tipped his hat and turned around to begin playing again. James was a man who lived alone, who had lost his family and his ability to communicate with words. Despite these difficulties James had in his daily life, he still could communicate with music.

Everyone has talent to offer, but we might not know enough about them to understand what that talent is. We tend to respond to those with their hands up first, clamoring for attention and we miss the quiet people who could help in a way the others could not.

James initially began visiting the church because of Dad's commitment to mission work, and this posed an awkward problem for the change effort. When James rocked and laughed down the aisle, it created fear among those that were already uncomfortable with the changes that had been made in the church. Sharing the mission stories of those people we helped outside of the church was fine, but James was not homebound. He was walking down the aisle of the church, awkwardly laughing his way into our personal space.

While he began as a point of contention, the church members gradually became protective of James. We started to see him the way Dad saw him, and while Dad got permission to share the story of his musical talent with the church, James would never play in front of anybody but Dad. I think that's because he was there for Dad. James did not ask for anything, but he became a touchstone for Dad during the toughest part of his change mission.

Sometimes, a smaller moment is saved for the key change warrior driving the transition, as a whisper from the universe that the direction taken is right. Believe me, change warriors doubt themselves when more people are irritated than satisfied, and the messy middle is all that can be seen. In those moments, big ideas and obvious skills aren't needed.

Sometimes we need a defibrillator, a physical representation of the heart of the change that reignites the sinus rhythm. James was a shining reminder that missions matter, and that everybody has something to give back, whether it is classical music or their teeth.

CHANGE LESSONS

When change comes with a name, it can be uncomfortable.

Sometimes your change effort can be represented by one individual who creates fear around the direction. Maybe the guy that leads the new sales training talks too loud, or the software systems lead talks over everybody's head. During change transition, people are extremely sensitive to anything that seems to represent a part of the change they don't really want. James was that point of discomfort, and Dad knew it. But, instead of stepping away from the individual, it's the change warrior's job to listen for the talent. Search for their story, and share that story with the rest of the team. Perhaps the sales guy brings an energy nobody else can. Maybe the technology woman has an intricate knowledge of the system that others lack. Find their music. Then share it with the team.

Sometimes the change warrior needs to listen for inspiration.

Change is difficult, and during transition it is messy and exhausting. The change warrior and disciples need to take some time, get quiet and look for what might be a gift in the toughest situations. That person who stood up in a meeting and told you he hated your sales program (which happened to me) might just become the catalyst for why the change must happen. The individual who brought up everything wrong with the new system might just help that system improve. And sometimes there is a person who represents the change others don't want but is there to help the change warrior remember that behind every change is a driving, passionate purpose.

"We make a living by what we get, but we make a life by what we give." —Winston Churchill

CHAPTER 18
MRS. ROBINSON AND WASPS

E verything during change feels like an obstacle. When people don't want something to happen, or when something feels threatening, it becomes an unknown, and the brain hates unknowns. Therefore, a change warrior must find ways to diffuse the pressure and allow people to laugh when the unexpected, unplanned and uncoordinated efforts occur.

I remember one Sunday when my dad was in the middle of his morning prayer. He stood at the pulpit, asked everyone to "please bow your heads for prayer," and then stayed silent for about ten seconds. Dad often provided that moment, allowing people time to disconnect from the world and connect to God. During these moments of silence, I always kept my eyes open as a kid, watching for those adults who would get uncomfortable and look up to make sure their eyes were supposed to still be closed. Of course, they'd then see me in the first pew with my head turned around staring at them, and they'd briefly looked panicked and quickly closed their eyes again. I believe that was one of the few times that I abused my power as a preacher's kid. Others would suddenly get a case of TB, coughing up a lung in their discomfort. Then there was the inevitable crinkling of candy paper from our older members from the local retirement center.

In one memorable meditative moment, Dad had reached the end of his silent entry ramp to prayer, and then started with specific prayers for those in the community. As he spoke to God, we started to hear some kind of faint music in the background. Suddenly, many people in the congregation were looking up, wondering if God was providing dramatic background music. The music faded, so people bowed their heads again. What we didn't realize was that the back of the sanctuary had a room that included a radio and a series of wires that connected to the front speakers. Apparently, someone left the radio on, and the wires of the radio connected with the wires of the speaker. What resulted was a moment Dad never expected.

As he prayed for those in the community that needed God's strength, the music grew louder, and louder, and louder. Suddenly, Dad's prayer was emphatically accompanied by Simon & Garfunkel in the middle of the song "Mrs. Robinson," right at the most appropriate verse of all . . .

And here's to you, Mrs. Robinson, Jesus loves you more than you will know, wo wo wo . . .

Dad didn't miss a beat. He simply continued his prayer, saying "And Lord, please be with Mrs. Robinson and all the Mrs. Robinson's of the world that need you . . ." His tone changed and reflected the smile that spread across his face (of course I had my eyes open, so I saw him). And then he said "amen," looked at the congregation, and started to laugh. Once he gave everyone permission to enjoy the gaff, everyone started to laugh, kicked off by my mother at the organ who had a distinctive, guffawing laugh that was contagious. I can't remember exactly what he said, but it made us laugh even harder. I think it was something like, "God has good taste in music." The church had been battling through a year of change, and we were smack dab in the middle of transition when the congregation shrunk and the problems grew. There were fewer people to help, so everyone was kicking in extra time in addition to their day jobs. As a result, Dad let everyone laugh because he knew if you can't laugh during change, you're in big trouble. Laughter alleviates stress and makes some ridiculous battles seem, well, ridiculous.

One of our favorite family stories happened when my brother, sister and I were very young. Dad was speaking to a congregation in a small country church in the middle of summer. The church had no air conditioning, and it was about 85 degrees outside with 100% humidity. Mom said it was like being inside a giant humidifier. The good news was that if anybody had croup, they were cured by the end of the service. These were the days when "air conditioning" consisted of funeral fans in every pew. Nothing was worse than sitting in a pew and realizing after the service started, that your pew had a plethora of hymnals, tiny pencils and visitors cards, but no funeral fans. Middle-aged women were known to ask a deacon very loudly for a fan if needed during the sermon. Now that I've experienced hot flashes, I have a deep respect for those women.

I still remember the exact look of those fans. The handle looked like a giant Popsicle stick, with a piece of square cardboard glued to it that had a picture of a pale, glowing Jesus knocking on a wooden door on one side and the name of the funeral home that had donated the fans to the church on the other. I always stared at Jesus, feeling he looked more like a savior hailing from Sweden than Bethlehem.

On this particular breath-suckingly hot Sunday, Dad stood at the pulpit delivering his sermon. The choir was located behind the minister, and my mom was a soprano and physically short, which meant she got the front row position. Dad had been speaking for about ten minutes and was reaching the emotional peak of his message. As Dad's voice elevated with emphasis, Mom zeroed in on something moving slowly up his neck. Unfortunately for Dad, it was a wasp.

You have to appreciate my mother's fear of insects that sting to understand her next move. Let's put it this way—my grandmother completely undressed at a church gathering when a bumblebee got in her dress, and Mother had inherited the gene. She was a woman of action with an absolute terror of anything in the bee family. As Dad reached the pinnacle of his message, Mom was locked in on the wasp and took action, picking up the hymnal from in front of her with both hands. Like a hired sniper setting her site, she kept her eyes on the wasp, raised both hands over her head, and reared back for maximum force. From a distance of only about twelve feet, my little mother reached back with all of her past-softball-wielding strength and let that hymnal fly towards my dad's neck.

That hymnal pounded my unsuspecting dad in the back of the head with all the force of Mom's terror, shocking him into complete silence. He turned slowly to look at her, who, in her defense and her Arkansas drawl, said, "It was a WASP!" Dad rubbed his head and said, "Good grief, Sue, I thought I had been struck by the Spirit!" The congregation, still quiet from the shock of the moment, burst into laughter. Dad looked at the congregation with his half-smile and said "I'm not going to recover from this. Everybody gets to go to lunch early today." The service ended, and Dad went home to ice his head, while Mom declared victory since Dad had not been stung by the wasp.

Change pushes us out of our comfort zone into anger, blame and chaos. There is no avoiding the build-up of emotion, and during transition it can sometimes feel breath-suckingly exhausting. Laughter and fun are the only way to take extreme emotion and channel it in a positive way, even if it requires a hymnal to the head.

CHANGE LESSONS

Change requires a release.

Researchers have said that what is often seen as resistance to change is actually just exhaustion. During transition, when new is coming but not there yet, and the old is leaving but not gone yet, every moment takes extra effort. Until change completes the emotional process and becomes the new point of comfort, it requires a constant sense of awareness on the part of the person experiencing the change. It's as if the primitive side of humans is looking for any potential threat in the jungle of this unknown territory. This tension can't build indefinitely, and eventually, exhaustion will set in.

Humor offers a quick vacation.

Milton Berle once said, "Laughter is [like] an instant vacation." If change keeps tension high, then people need a release or they will wear out before the change is complete. Laughter is a way of saying, "we will survive this change, and we will thrive because we're stronger than anything it can throw our way." Physically, laughter releases endorphins that make people feel better and calmer. In fact, you might notice that when something funny occurs during a time of change, audiences sometimes over-laugh. Why? Because laughter offers a way of releasing stress without crying. Tears contain stress hormones, so whether you laugh until you cry or simply start with crying, you are letting it all go. Here are some ways to ensure humor is a part of the change effort:

- The executive sponsor not only commits to the change but lets people know they are as uncomfortable as the rest of the team by sharing a funny story about discomfort with something new.
- The change warrior admits most people will wish they would go away, but like a bad penny they will keep showing up until change starts to happen.
- Stumbles are celebrated with "Trip Awards" handed out weekly. People share their stories while others vote on the greatest trip of the week. Why? Because stumbles mean people are trying.
- Don't take everything too seriously. Some of the change will stick, some will not, so celebrate the steps forward and make it about the people.

As the change warrior, you have to be the tough messenger holding a box of tissues - pushing folks through discomfort while acknowledging that fears and tears are an acceptable part of the process. And when tears come from laughter? Even better.

"We cannot really love anybody with whom we never laugh." –Agnes Repplier

CHAPTER 19
SQUEEZING TITHE OUT OF A TURNIP

E ven during the toughest times of change there might be a point where a leader has to ask for more support out of resources who have already committed much of their time and energy to the change effort. At least once or twice a year in the Southern Baptist church, ministers must address what we call "the tithe," or the money people in the church give to keep the church moving. Without tithing, Baptist churches can be challenged to keep their doors open.

But tithe is voluntary, and many people were willing to show up on Sunday and get their spiritual food, but were reluctant to give their money to support the church itself. Money is probably the only topic that I discovered was more loaded than personal faith. Everybody loves the church until you ask them to put something in the offering plate to support the classes and sermons they take advantage of, but somehow feel God should be funding. Mom and Dad would hear things such as, "I give my time." Sounds impressive, except most of those who didn't give offering also didn't give any of their time other than claiming their pew on Sunday and their spot at the local steakhouse after the service. The irony is that those who could least afford to give were frequently the ones who would give more. And Dad knew their situation and couldn't allow the burden to fall on their shoulders.

We do that sometimes during change. We find the disciples who are already exhausted and ask them to lead more efforts. They are asked to lead a Sunday School class, be on the Vacation Bible School committee, sing in the choir and volunteer in the nursery. We ask too much of the willing because we know they will.

So, Dad would reluctantly give the "budget sermon." He hated asking for money, and he understood that asking for more from people was a potential tripwire. At the point of transition, your population is shrinking as the Rabbits have hopped to a more entertaining environment, and those remaining are either unhappy core families waiting for you to leave or exhausted disciples just wanting a few weeks off.

Dad would stand up to preach, and only we knew what was coming and why Dad looked like he was getting ready to vomit. We'd look around and see everybody in the congregation with their eyes on Dad, ready to have their spiritual tanks filled for the week. Then suddenly, Dad would mention tithe and faces suddenly looked like balloons that had a slow leak, deflating with disappointment. Once it sunk in that they were trapped for the tithe sermon, men would start choking while their wives looked down to dig through their purses looking for cough drops. Those on the budget committee would squirm in their seats, hoping nobody would personally blame them for the report that resulted in this thirty minutes of pain.

Dad always started his budget sermons with an apology—letting the congregants know that he was as uncomfortable with this topic as they were. But it still had to be discussed, or some staff member or church program would have to end. He always thanked everyone for what they had already done and tried to find a way to show his appreciation while continuing to ask for more.

A key obstacle to change occurs when people who are tired have to be asked to give just a little bit more. We always knew that those who had been selfish with their money up to that point would remain stingy no matter what was said, and those that had already committed would commit even more. The same was true for those who provided effort and time. The only way Dad could preach a budget sermon was to remind himself why it was important to the mission of the church, and remind the congregation of the heart of the goal—the people who would be reached and helped.

It's at these points that change warriors must return to the beginning, and associate the movement with something bigger than each individual. People must believe that what they're doing is worth the sacrifice and time, and a rousing speech won't do it. If a leader isn't truly passionate about their commitment and the change effort, it will be felt. And, by the way, if a true goal was not communicated at the beginning of the change—or if the true goal only benefits a few people —you won't survive this obstacle.

CHANGE LESSONS

Some change messages are hard to deliver, no matter what the topic.

There will come a time, as in any endeavor, where the "ask" seems too big. Whether it be asking for more money, energy, or resources, the request for additional effort from exhausted disciples can be difficult. But the resources must be delivered and there is always a financial truth to change that can't be avoided. The hard part is that sometimes you have to ask for even more out of them than they've already delivered. And what they've been willing to do has been above and beyond the expectations. The change leader who has to ask is tired as well, but we have more to give than we realize. We can get through it. But the request has to come first.

Build tough messages on the heart of the original goal.

Followers have stayed faithful because they believe in the original goal. If they have only been following because they've been forced to, then tough messages can mean a complete mental disconnect from the effort. Make sure the original goal has been communicated and still inspires before delivering the tough message.

"Good communication is as stimulating as black coffee, and just as hard to sleep after." –Anne Morrow Lindbergh

CHAPTER 20
BETTY AND HER BIBLE

Y ou know the transition phase of change is slowing when a few people start coming back, and those in place start seeing the purpose of the change happening and succeeding. Once a leader or change warrior has worked through most of the transition phase, the change is about to get really exciting because they're getting ready to see results. Every cliché in the world ("It's darkest before the dawn," "The lowest ebb is before the tide," etc.) is true. Just when you think the change isn't going to happen or isn't worth the effort, there is a turn. But there's always a final fear that clings to the effort that shows itself just as the turn to new reality begins.

In one church where Dad had worked for two years to instill a mission-outreach within the community, the journey to that place of change where everything starts to shine was almost thwarted by a woman we'll call Betty. While many of our new members were part of the outreach program, they were members who were likable and who added value. Dad always said that it was easy to love those who are easy to love, but the true test was to love the unlovable. Betty was our own change SAT.

Change remains delicate until it is integrated. Simply installing new behaviors and explicit instructions isn't even close to integration.

The behaviors have to become a part of the organization, living and breathing through each individual employee. And even as these behaviors have been spotlighted, positively reinforced, and even worked into performance reviews until the majority of employees and leaders are on board, any proof of potential failure can pull back the Rabbits and the Turtles who constitute the majority of your organization. And the change can fail. Betty was that potential proof.

Betty lived in the apartment complex behind the church with her teenage son (a heroin addict) and her six-year-old who we will call Lou. Let me tell you, Lou was a treat for the eyes and the ears. He and Betty rarely bathed and had a talent for talking during the church service in volumes that should be saved for a rock concert. Their entrance was always five minutes after the service started, and usually during the morning prayer. Lou would burst down the aisle as if he had been shot from a very large rubber band. Walking behind him was Betty screaming "LOU—SLOW DOWN!" in a deep, guttural, voice that could navigate a ship through any fog.

She carried with her the family bible—a bible placed in a wooden case that must have been taken directly from the biggest bibles on earth museum. She generally wore a large flowered house dress with white athletic socks and large black shoes. We didn't judge her by her clothes, since none of us had much money either. It was when she yelled out things like "LOU, ZIP UP YOUR ZIPPER" in the middle of the sermon that we tended to get a little annoyed. Or when Lou would take off his incredibly dirty socks and throw them at you during prayer, or when Lou would run up and grab Dad around the waist while he tried to preach, hanging on like a barnacle.

Just like James, Betty provided a bit of a challenge to Dad's mission-focused change effort. Congregants looked at each other every time she walked in as if to say, "Is this the change our leader is encouraging? Do we really want more Bettys?" And, of course, she was there whenever the church doors were open. She was devoted to Dad and the church, something we wished, selfishly, was not the case.

I remember the night that we were meeting to visit new members or those that had requested a visit and at the tender age of twelve, it was my first visitation! I was partnered with a young woman named

Karen who was a cute, funny college student who would make a very cool visitation partner. People would LOVE us.

As Karen and I prepared to walk out of the church door to go visit, I heard my dad say, "Donna—could you come here, please?" At the last possible moment, Betty had shown up for visitation. Dad felt that he would probably be the only person comfortable visiting others with a draw like Betty, and he knew that he shouldn't visit with another female alone (just being cautious). My intuition told me that my fun evening was getting ready to shift. So, I walked with tremendous trepidation toward Dad to hear these words. "Donna, I need you to visit with Betty and me tonight. I'm sorry." I'm sure the "DAD!!!" rang through the fellowship hall. Luckily, Betty was busy pulling up her mismatching knee-hi's and belching simultaneously, so she didn't hear me.

I spent a long evening listening to Betty say unimaginable things to potential new members like, "My son is on heroin. How old is your son?" But I survived, and the day we visited Betty's apartment, I saw the poverty from which she came and the abusive anger of her teenage son and realized her life was a nightmare. And, yet, she wanted to do good work.

She was trying to give to others when she really had so little to give. The day she brought a plant from her apartment to give to my dad for his office was especially touching. Unfortunately, it was her teenage son's marijuana, which I'm sure made him even angrier, but Betty thought it was just a really nice plant that smelled nice.

Even when she threatened his change efforts, Dad always defended Betty. The threat wasn't as much about her as it was about our judgment of her, our desire to have sermons free of dirty socks and Betty's booming voice. She was a poster child for the love Dad asked us to give, and most of us were not nearly as much like Jesus as we should have been. Eventually, the fear turned to a realization that while we said we could love anybody, we really had to work at it. Just because you're serving a greater good, doesn't make it easy; sometimes the toughest work in the world involves service to others.

We learned that you can't judge without knowing the story behind the situation, that even when we know the story we might still hope for a moment when we can shut the doors and close out whatever makes us uncomfortable. Most of all, we learned that the change we were asking to be part of was difficult, but it had a purpose. The day that Betty shared some of her story with the church, we all cried. We felt her pain. And Betty went from being the toughest part of change to the definition of it, and we were better because of her.

CHANGE LESSONS

Change warriors defend the integrity of the change, even when it's not shiny.

Not every element of change is going to be a "wow, see how much better things are" kind of moment. Sometimes you have to look at a part of change that isn't particularly charismatic or appealing, and the change warrior has to be able to still defend the change and maintain a commitment to it. This is called leadership, and the confidence of the leader will determine if the followers hold tight until the change is complete.

The toughest change characters might end up being your greatest asset.

At first, Betty seemed to be an obstacle to the change effort. Her mere existence in the church and interruptions during it caused members to pull back supporting a more mission-focused approach. She literally represented everything that the congregation most feared, including new members who were different and caused others to be uncomfortable. But when her passion for the church was revealed through commitment, and when people decided to get to know her, she became the very reason the change had integrity. She was the reason for the work.

"The only safe ship in a storm is leadership." –Faye Wattleton

CHAPTER 21
BAPTISMS, NEW BEGINNINGS AND TIDAL WAVES

I have a terrible confession to make—my least favorite event as a Southern Baptist are baptisms. Full-immersion is an important part of the Baptist faith for which many founding leaders died (it's all in the name), but I have developed post-baptism stress disorder having witnessed probably more than a thousand baptisms in my lifetime. In the church, baptism is the pinnacle of experiences. It is a change in life and commitment in full view. Unfortunately, there are also other things in full view when people rise out of the water in white baptismal robes that are wet and clingy.

Most of our churches had a baptismal that was located behind the choir loft. The average baptismal is approximately four feet deep, and looks a lot like a tiny swimming pool. Many past Baptist ministers baptized in rivers, as my grandfather (also a Baptist minister) did. My mom told me of one baptismal service where he baptized several people while housing a fish hook in his heel. There were slimy stones that caused slippage and moss floating up the gowns. That's why baptismals were created.

Baptismals vary, but they are usually either a small pool jutting out from the wall and standing alone, or they are positioned in an elevated area behind the choir loft. From the vantage point behind the choir, there were stairways coming from both the left and the right. One led to the women's dressing room and the other to the men's dressing room. Most baptisms are conducted at the beginning of the service so the preacher can baptize, get cleaned up during hymns and the offerings, and walk in ready for the sermon.

Because I have a sincere dread of what might happen during a baptism, I remember every sound and sight. Walking into the church on a baptismal Sunday morning, you see the water against the glass partition located at the front of the baptismal. When the organ stops playing and the service begins, you hear the sound of water moving as the minister comes down the stairs. My dad used to wear rubber hipsters—I always thought those were cool when I was a kid...I thought he looked like a firefighter. Anyway, my stomach would always tighten when I heard my dad wading down the stairs because I knew baptism couldn't be far behind.

Once Dad stood in his black robe and made a few comments, then the first of the converted would venture timidly into the water. You could hear them on the first step, second step, picking up speed on the third step and then gasping on the fourth because they were not prepared for how cold the water would get since the baptismal was filled around 6:00 a.m. Once they regained their composure, they would make eye contact with Dad and hold his gaze as if he were a lighthouse on a stormy night. Their arms would float on top of the water, and they would try to move smoothly and seem confident, but that's hard to do when you're in a robe that is now either floating up to your waist while the glass you were approaching went down to your thighs. Like you weren't vulnerable enough already.

Once the person reached Dad's extended arm, they would be turned to face the congregation. The silence always unnerved me, as did the looks on people's faces. Their expressions were generally not joyous, but focused on how they would go straight into the water, back first, without any sign of panic. It was like a trust exercise combined with all of the possibilities of white robes that would get wet and expose rolls of extra ice cream, hidden tattoos or the thick undergarments of those who were prepared for exposure.

These were people making a commitment to something new, and I often witnessed a major change in their lives. You go into that water as one person and come out as a new creation. I loved the symbolism of baptism, but I just didn't like the baptism itself. I took swimming lessons at the YMCA when I was eight years-old, and my instructor was ex-military and lacked the understanding required to work with a child who wasn't comfortable in water. At one point, as I hit four-feet, I went under three times, yelling a gurgled "help" when I would surface. Our instructor made the entire class, including my older sister, watch my humiliation without offering any help. I finally sat on the bottom of the pool waiting for sweet death when my sister walked out and saved me (I was really short for my age). Since that moment, any time water is over my head I panic. Let's just say that when I'm in water no dove lands on my shoulder and as I flail, I'm pretty sure that I'm not the daughter with whom God is well pleased.

And sometimes, that is how change is—we'd like to get the result, but we don't want to flail and be made vulnerable in the process. We want our older sister to come save us from what our brain is screaming might be certain death. We don't want to admit that maybe some of the work we've done in the past wasn't the best, or is no longer relevant. We want a new start, without the public commitment.

And sometimes the public commitment goes awry. I had a friend whose father was getting ready to baptize a rather large woman who was not aware undergarments should still be worn with their robe. When she came out of the water, I think there were spiritual experiences all over the place. On the bright side, the bored congregation members were now paying attention. That's why most churches have deacons assigned to each dressing area—to eliminate the potential wet t-shirt effect.

My mom remembers a baptism that a minister friend of hers experienced. A man in his church was the size of an NFL linebacker, and he actually got stuck in the very narrow stairway leading to the baptismal. They had to squirt soap around him and on the walls, and then use several deacons to push from behind. When he was finally set free, he flew into the baptismal and did a belly flop that sent a tidal wave over the choir. Since this was in the fifties, there were a lot of flattened bouffants and false eyelashes crawling down faces like drowned caterpillars.

Baptisms wake up congregations, not always because of the inspiration but because of the potential for stumbles. Due to my YMCA experience, I have learned to hate walking by a public pool and hearing the kids splashing. Wave pools freak me out. I formulated a future dislike for water parks, and I totally blame my parents for being Baptists. My Presbyterian friends were sprinkled as children, which I thought was a brilliant strategy. Instead, at the tender age of eight, I had to relive the YMCA experience in front of the entire congregation. The best news was that my dad would be holding me, and I trusted him implicitly.

On the big morning, I peeked out from behind the curtain when it was my turn, and waded out where my dad was waiting and smiling. The water was cold, and my need to be funny (particularly when nervous) almost resulted in an impromptu comedy performance. But I stayed serious, stood up on the provided corner cement step (for short people) and folded my right arm so that my hand rested on my shoulder (as instructed). Dad said a few words that I did not hear because I kept sucking in air thinking it was time to hold my breath. When the time came to "dip," I had almost hyperventilated.

Finally, Dad said those magic words with his left hand in the air —"In the name of the Father, the Son, and the Holy Spirit, Amen." As I fell backward and smelled the water getting closer, I instinctively reached out and grabbed my dad around the neck. He almost went down with me. Coming out of the water, my conversion experience became an intense focus on getting air. Once my head was completely out of the water, I felt an incredible sense of relief, and I waded to the safety of the dressing room as quickly as possible.

For many, baptism was exactly what it should have been—a public commitment to a life changed by love. During any change, there comes a moment when not only is a person on board for the journey, but they are willing to tell everyone they are all-in, even when it's not popular with colleagues, friends or family members. It takes courage and an absolute belief in the direction being taken. It means an acceptance of whatever is before them, happy or sad, good or bad.

Commitments to the new signify acceptance and growth. And leaders can determine a successful transition by the number of people who are willing to be completely on board because they're dedicated to a new direction.

CHANGE LESSONS

Remember that change does not have equal appeal.

While for some the act of baptism is a moving and spiritual experience, for others, it's a time to choke on water in front of a crowd with a white robe clinging to you. But here's the thing to remember—every change in churches or organizations goes through the filter of each individual's fears and hopes. Some changes are okay with some but terrify others. A great change warrior understands that they have to watch individual reactions, and determine how to get each person to move through their fears and to the ultimate change.

Find ways to help followers jump back on board the new reality.

Once you've moved to the exciting part of change, that part where the fear has been overcome and the new ideas are starting to make a positive difference, you need to find ways to show the commitment of new followers. Even though a change warrior might be frustrated by those "hoppers" who left during change (even mentally) and are trying to reengage, they need to be forgiven. Not many people have the courage to wade into change and come out the other side. They prefer to simply wait, and they need an exciting way to reengage once they're ready.

"How lovely to think that no one need wait a moment, we can start now, start slowly changing the world!" –Anne Frank

CHAPTER 22
SUNRISE BREAKTHROUGHS

My favorite holiday was always Easter Sunday. Not just because of the victorious message tied to the holiday, but because it seemed that Easter has always been represented both metaphorically and literally by allowing our emergence from the darkest part of change. Whether it was coincidental timing or just the hope that the sunshine of spring brings, Easter seemed to always be our turning point.

There is something about a holiday which celebrates a new beginning and victory over struggle. No matter what your religious belief is, that kind of celebration is the best. Easter is lilies, love, and sunrises. It reminds us that darkness and storms only last so long. Eventually, the light shines and its warmth is felt in every fiber of your being, only because you thought you'd never feel it again.

Any Baptist Easter morning worth its salt starts with a sunrise service where everybody drags in with curlers still in their hair to watch the sun slowly peek over the horizon like a bud, then spring into full bloom as we stand, pajama-clad, in honor of its glory. We come in shivering from the cold and leave with goosebumps and are delivered by the beauty of hope. I never understood sunrise services held indoors because that service is a lose/lose. You just have to get up at the break of dawn to stand inside and stare at your slippers. If it can't be outside, it shouldn't exist at all.

If you've never been to an outdoor sunrise service, let me paint you a picture. One of our churches out west had a parking lot that faced the mountains over which the sun would rise. So, about 5:30 a.m., the minister of music and his family would join us to roll the piano out into the parking lot and carry chairs and hymnals for the service. What made this most entertaining was the fact that my dad encouraged people to come in comfortable clothing, which is why Mom and the minister of the music's wife both had on their fuzzy slippers, robe, and curlers in their hair. My sister and I and the minister of music's two daughters did as well—those pink foam curlers that clipped in. My hair was thin at the time, so I always had at least one curler hanging at a weird angle threatening to fall out at any moment.

Little by little, cars filled with angry toddlers and exhausted adults would pull up. Kids held Easter baskets with fake grass clinging tenaciously to their cowboy and ballerina pajamas and robes. A few women would be dressed to the nines in their Easter finery, which we found ridiculous since they would inevitably have pancake syrup on them (the pancake breakfast followed the sunrise service) or be really wrinkled by the 11:00 service. After the ten or so loyal families arrived, we all positioned ourselves in the parking lot so we could watch the sun come up over the mountains. If you've ever lived in a desert area, it is really cold until the sun chooses to show itself, filling our bodies and souls with warmth. Whatever was being said, shared, sung or prayed would gain energy as soon as the sun started coming up. Our minister of music had a single trumpeter that really couldn't play too well, but it was a trumpet. He would signal the refrain of our favorite, victorious hymn. We would begin quietly, watching the sun (at complete danger to our corneas) come over the mountains. The hymn was named "Low in the Grave He Lay," and would start in respectful whispers:

Low in the Grave He Lay, Jesus my Savior,
Waiting the Coming Day, Jesus my Lord.

Then the piano would pick up the pace, and our less than talented lone trumpeter would kick in for emphasis as we all belted out the peppy refrain...

UP FROM THE GRAVE HE AROSE!

And I swear, it was in that refrain that people would start to smile and realize that the struggle was getting results, and the sun peeking over the magnificent mountains represented the light at the end of the tunnel. Instinctively, we would join hands and start to look like Cindy Lou Hoo and her friends in Whoville singing around the Christmas tree. By the third verse, we were basking in the warmth of the sun, our love for each other, sincere respect for our mission and the delicious pay-off after months of hard work and financial commitment.

Change, while not always dramatic, begins with dusk. The organization or individual facing the change is holding desperately to the light of day of the good times to avoid the inevitable night. And because we don't want to pay the price with clouds, we try to ignore them to look behind us at the remnants that remain. But life expands, and contracts, and there is no stopping the light or the dark. As transition ends and converts to a new reality, the sun begins to show itself.

Our "change" was now becoming our exciting, new reality, which is when all of the falling out of the nest and flapping of wings results in actual flying. Eventually, flying becomes the norm and a new baby bird of a problem is born, but for a while, it is glorious. Except for the change warrior. Because new reality means the change warrior's job is done, and it's time to move on.

CHANGE LESSONS

People must celebrate when the light of change begins to rise.

Every change effort, if led correctly, will eventually reach the point when there is more excitement and light than darkness and frustration. When this happens, a good change warrior knows to gather those that have helped lead, organize and commit to the change. These players should be allowed to come together, stand in a parking lot, or sit and have dinner, join hands and lift their glasses to toast each other. They managed to stay when the going was tough, now they deserve the opportunity to celebrate, if only for an evening. Of course, more change is always on the way, but if you fail to bask in the glow of success, people will be less likely to hang in there for the next change. There has to be an emotional pay-off.

Change will eventually become an exciting new reality.

The emotional process of change shows that while it begins in a place of comfort, emotions move us through anger, denial, numbness and chaos. If we choose to stay in chaos for a short period, there is a point at which it becomes everyone's new reality. Those are exciting times, where the pay-off is finally seen by those who stuck with it, and the many who refused to be a part of the change until it was proven are allowed to jump on board.Because whether people were onboard with change during the difficult stages, they have eventually left the nest. And in the new reality, the sun shines on everybody. And every partici-pant gets a chance to fly.

"Sadness flies on the wings of the morning, and out of the heart of darkness comes the light." –Jean Giraudoux

CHAPTER 23
BLEST BE THE TIE

The hardest part of being the child of a change warrior was leaving the church just as things were accelerating again. New people were joining, new money was being contributed, additions were being built and new signs were going up. This inevitably meant it was time to sing our family's closing hymn, "Blest Be the Tie."

In a déjà vu moment for us, Dad would call the deacons to the front of the church, recognizing those who had worked hard and been committed during the change effort. He would do a quick review of where we started, the change we had experienced and where we were now. Smiles would cover the faces of the congregation who felt this was some awesome statement that we had hit the new reality, and it was time to celebrate. Then Dad would join hands with the deacons, and in one instance said, "God's work is done through all of us. This chain is an important part of this church, but no link is more important than another. However, one of the links in this chain is going to be missing."

He then stepped out of the chain and joined the hands of the deacons that had been on either side of him. You'd hear gasps in the congregation, and people would try to make eye contact with us. We would look straight ahead, furious that Dad was bringing this much attention to a painful announcement. Then he'd finish with "The chain will be just as strong without this link, but Sue and I have decided to accept another call to a church that needs our help. You all are strong, and this church is ready to move forward with a new leader."

That line would bring out the handkerchiefs. Once, a large young man we all adored burst into sobs in the middle of the announcement and yelled, "Why? Why are you leaving me?" and everybody began to cry louder. As the situation escalated, Dad probably regretted the dramatic way he made the announcement. Eventually emotions were reined in, and midst sobs and sniffles, the entire congregation would join hands and sing "Blest be the Tie," which goes like this:

Blest be the tie that binds
Our hearts in Christian love;
The fellowship of kindred minds
Is like to that above.

If you're reading this and are protestant, you probably know this song. Many churches close every church service with it, having congregants join hands across the aisles.

Well, "Blest Be the Tie" became my family's swan song. I still get choked up when I have to join hands with the person next to me and sing it. There are tears of joy when new reality is reached, but there is also the reality that as one change closes, another begins. And a new phase often requires a new leader or a new consultant. The church now needed a leader who could build on the momentum. My parents were crisis ministers, coming in when the tide was the lowest and leaving once the truly difficult change had been completed.

My general finding has been that once change has been "completed," the person who was key during the difficult times gets associated with the pain, and will get restless when there is more maintenance than change.

It's like I told a manager once who wondered why in the world I was leaving a position that I had basically created and excelled in. He said, "Why would you do this? You have leadership's respect; you can write your own ticket and have this job as long as you want it. You're at the top of the mountain." I responded the most honest way I knew how by saying, "You know, the top of the mountain isn't what I love. It's the climb. When I'm at the top of the mountain, I'm not looking at the view. I'm looking for the next mountain."

And that was the calling that Dad had, one to help churches make the climb. And he sacrificed for it. Dad experienced some depression and dark days, so never expect that a change warrior comes out of the battle unscathed. But, once you do hit a new reality, there is no feeling like it. The most difficult thing is saying goodbye. You want the rest, you want to enjoy it, but you know that maintaining it is not your jam. When the offer of a raise comes and the prospect of a new car or better house tempts, just remember that change leaders would rather have a challenge than some extra change.

Plus, Dad had already accepted the next call after our prayer in the woods, and so continued our circle of life.

We'd pack up the U-Haul, climb in our latest car disaster, wave goodbye to our dearest change partners and hit the road. And we'd get the gift of our honeymoon period all over again, a little extra cash in our pocket and success in our soul.

CHANGE LESSONS

Change warriors know how to leave a strong chain.

Any change warrior that leaves behind a team that "can't make it without him or her" is not a good change warrior. The best agents know that when it's time to move on, whether it be a church or a project, the team left behind can lose a link and become even stronger. The job is done only when it can be done without the agent.

Change warriors recognize their need to move on.

A good change warrior understands when it's time to move on, and they know that no matter how great the offer is, staying behind and conducting maintenance is not what they do best. Not many people can deal with the second phase of change over and over again, but change warriors thrive on it because it is both their passion and strength. If they try to stay on the top of the mountain, they'll either a) get bored or b) stir things up and cannibalize their own change. As Willie Nelson sang, great change warriors know when they need to be "on the road again." Move on.

"Out of life's school of war: What does not destroy me, makes me stronger." –Friedrich Wilhelm Nietzsche

CHAPTER 24
THE FUTURE OF CHANGE

Most change is kicked off by extreme discomfort, usually financial in nature. It is something that causes organizations to reach out for help and recognize that a fix is required that they, obviously, need help with. Unfortunately, many of them wait too long to ask for help, determined that whatever they've done in the past will somehow, magically, begin to work. When they realize it's not going to happen, they bring in change consultants.

The good consultants will not just change how something is rolled out, they will come in and help create a culture that is ready to not only innovate but to become, in many ways, a better organization. The elite change warriors have an intuitive element to their work; they tend to sense who is on board, who isn't, and who will help the change move. They might change direction when something isn't working, even though other leaders will fight to keep things according to plan. Intuition and using a sixth sense about what happens next are essential to real change warriors.

Watching my parents, I learned that real change will be scary, painful and inspiring. That nothing good comes easy. That real leadership isn't afraid to be unpopular. I worry about change programs that have fancy acronyms and are implemented by any project team minus the change warrior leader who will make the difference between implementation and integration. I worry about projects that are kicked off, partially rolled out, and then stopped so the next change can start. I think people have learned to distrust change, because of that reason. They wait for it to pass instead because they've lost too much energy implementing change that was left behind in the name of an organizational attention deficit disorder we call change management.

Most of all, I worry about organizations that forget the people who have made them great, mediocre or worse. It is the heartbeat behind the organization that determines its future health no matter how automated it becomes. There are people selling, people buying, and people who want to be a part of it, but only if they know the why, the how and the what. Since they are putting in the effort and time, they deserve to know every bit of that.

My family made our last church transition in 1976, moving back to the place we started. It was a fun journey, with lessons of its own. We had three teenagers in an AMC Hornet Hatchback, traveling from California to Virginia. Some of you might not remember the AMC Hornet Hatchback, but let me fill you in. It looked like a Ford Pinto met a Gremlin and they had a very unattractive child. It fits approximately four small adults comfortably.

In our Hornet Hatchback, we had two men who were 6' ft tall, three 5'2" women, a small dog that carried a ridiculous amount of weight on her tiny frame, a Coleman ice chest for breakfast and lunch stops, a thermos and two suitcases. Add to this the ukulele and melodica (musical instruments necessary for cross-country singing), a tape recorder (we recorded the trip for those in the church that wanted to hear us sing badly) and a stack of maps that took up considerable room as once opened, we never folded them back up.

We had six days to make the trip to Virginia, and very little money to do it. We packed our breakfasts and lunches in the Coleman ice chest, had a thermos full of iced tea, and then treated ourselves to dinner in the less than enchanting motels we stopped at along the road. Our big treat was that once, in Yuma, Arizona, we each got a soda pop at the rest stop. I chose a Fanta™ Orange in a glass bottle, and ran to the restroom first so I could savor my drink. When I got back to the rest stop picnic table, the soda had evaporated in the 124 degree heat. I was both devastated and suspect that my brother drank it.

Our trip to Virginia included singing ("Edelweiss" and "Swing Low Sweet Chariot" were favorites), laughing, sleeping, occasional cursing (me) and constant gas (the dog—we swear). Occasionally, we treated ourselves to a stop at a Stuckeys…Mom loved their pecan logs, and we would each get some inexpensive candy.

Basically, we had eight hours a day in the car with little air-conditioning and a lot of bodies. We were wrinkled, hot and whoever was stuck in the very back of the car with the Coleman chest for the longest period needed a lot of Advil. This was before seat belts were required in cars, and my sister and I took turns curling up in the fetal position in the hatchback area with the glass of the hatchback closing down on us like a bad attic ceiling that magnified the desert sun. Eventually, I had to be back there the most because my sister was very pale and sunburned easily. She lucked out.

While back there I read multiple books and thought about a guy I left behind that I didn't really like until the day we left. He had given me a necklace that was basically a rock on a chain. I wore it as if it were the Hope Diamond and created a relationship in my mind that did not exist at all. We all did whatever it took to get through eight long hours a day, but we had fun. There was no pressure because our last change was complete, and we were in change warrior heaven, which involved lots of dreaming about how great our next change would be.

Since either a) the car wasn't air-conditioned or b) we kept the air conditioning off because of gas consumption, or c) we kept the windows down because of the dog's gas, we suffered through the state of Texas. For you Texans, forgive me, but my exact line after a full day of driving was, "Are we in hell or Texas?" Half of our trip was trying to get through that state, and man was it hot! But we held onto our mirage of the next church, dreaming about what it would be like, how cute the boys would be, what our house would look like and how everyone would act and dress. Once again, we savored the in-between of change.

On our last day of travel to a new location, there was a noticeable change of mood in our car. The air seemed a little more electric as we would pile in the car. There was a little less chatter and a little more introspection. We started looking out of our respective windows, noticing the change in the trees, the condition of the roads and the signs that welcomed us to our new home. I, of course, was looking at the sky since I was crammed in the very back of the car, but just as introspective.

While we loved California, we were now making it full circle back to the state from which we had started our first big trip eight years earlier. After years of living in beautiful, sunny California, we had forgotten about the green of the Blue Ridge Mountains. Our home in Southern California had cactus in the front yard, clover in the back, rocks on our roof and cow skulls as our decoration. Our 7-Elevens had stucco walls, our gas stations were tired from overuse, and our school playgrounds were paved. In California, land is hard to find, though the weather absolutely rocks and the people are kind.

As we passed the "Welcome to Virginia" sign, we began talking again. My family rarely stays pensive for long—we always move to humor as quickly as possible. And the more nervous we become, the funnier we tend to be. We stopped for gas at one point and were amazed that the gas station was covered in brick with flowers along the side of it and had a clean little restaurant inside of it. Then, we saw what would be our reassurance that life was going to be good in Virginia...a 7-Eleven that looked like a little house. "It's so cute!" we all exclaimed.

We were avoiding talking about the uncomfortable parts of our new destination. It was Christmas break, my sister would be starting a new college, my brother would enter middle school and I would be starting the second semester of my sophomore year in high school. I already dreaded the first day, walking in the doors having no idea where you are but fully aware of everybody staring your way. Lunch was always the worst, as you try to fill an hour looking as if you belong. But today, this day, we sang one more hymn together, we laughed and we thanked heaven for that little 7-Eleven.

Today was our day. We had a little more time to enjoy the in-between, and prepare for the honeymoon phase. We had Mom and Dad, the dog and each other. We were neither popular nor unpopular. It was time to keep singing, and relaxing. Tomorrow we would prepare for our new change. And thus goes the life of a change warrior.

CHANGE LESSONS

Preparing for the next change requires a break.

Even though the last phase of a positive change is an exhilarating one after surviving phase two, change warriors still need a break before they begin working in a new environment. Our trip provided us with approximately eight days of relaxation, laughter and anticipation. What we left behind had been healed and where we had to go remained unknown. We huddled together in our Hornet and enjoyed the peace of no responsibility.

Dreams of the next improvement drives change warriors.

Every change warrior has one purpose—to improve something or someone. Whether it be weight loss, project completion or instilling a new sales culture, change warriors love to improve. The best agents know that when they leave their latest project, they should utilize their "high" to dream of their next conquest. The only sad change warrior is the one without a dream and without the next mountain to climb. Their greatest joy is breaking a pattern of stagnation and infusing energy, elevating the current status to something new and better. By the way, great change warriors do not subscribe to change for the sake of change. If there's no improvement, they will feel that they have failed.

"When patterns are broken, new worlds emerge." –Tuli Kupferberg

CHAPTER 25
FINAL CHANGE LESSONS

Whether you are a minister, a student leader or a CEO, leading change requires that you face the discomfort of change and charge forward when everybody else is holding back. To succeed, you have to be willing to plan your strategy, find your disciples, accelerate early to gain momentum, lose people when it gets uncomfortable, and leave when success is being celebrated.

You must remember not to be seduced by the siren call of your comfort zone, deal with your own anger and denial so others don't see it, sit in chaos and let it wash over you, and then lead everyone into the new reality. I have no doubt that Moses wasn't always sure of himself, but those following him were sure that he was.

Change is eternal; our ability to lead people through it is not required but always necessary. Focusing on processes and projects is controllable and offers spreadsheets that guide us through each step. But people are the heartbeat of the change; they will make or break it, and yet they are ignored. To drive real change, to move an organization, you have to be able to move people. And, even then, you'll be surprised by their responses. Because people, unlike processes, are not predictable.

So, take the lessons I've shared and then buckle up...it's going to be a bumpy ride. Enjoy the climb, because once it's over, if you're truly a change warrior, you'll be looking for that next mountain. Life is not about concessions, it's about challenges. It's not about loss, it's about improvement. The people are what you will remember, the people form the collective soul of every business. Be willing to be the person who sacrifices his or her own comfort to improve the life of someone else, or improve the environment of a company. If you're reading this book, then this is your call, no matter what level you are in the organization. Your change leadership might be informal, from the middle-out or the bottom-up. No matter what your position, you have a call. Accept it, commit to it, and go make the world a better place!

"The important thing is this: to be able at any moment to sacrifice what we are for what we would become." –Charles DuBois

ABOUT THE AUTHOR

Donna Strother Highfill is both a corporate change warrior and storyteller. She has worked with corporate organizations for over thirty years helping them maneuver challenging change while moving people and improving performance. She is the author of four books and hundreds of published blogs and articles. Donna uses stories, humor, and influence to teach and inspire her audience as facilitator and speaker. She is President of Donna Highfill Consulting, LLC, based in Richmond, VA.

ALSO BY
DONNA STROTHER HIGHFILL

Real People, Real Change: Stories of a Change Warrior in the Business World

Glitter Girl

Medium-ish: Stories of a normal woman with a paranormal life

REFERENCES

Chapter 1, First You Must Know Without Knowing

7-Eleven is a trademark of 7-Eleven, Inc.

"A Quote by Dean Koontz." Goodreads. Goodreads. Accessed May 5, 2022. https://www.goodreads.com/quotes/95562-intuition-is-seeing-with-the-soul.

Myers-Briggs is a trademark of Myers & Briggs Foundation.

Nimrod is a trademark of Ward Manufacturing, Inc.

Peck, M. Scott. *People of the Lie*. Touchstone, 1998.

Swiss Army Knife is a trademark of Victornox AG.

Chapter 2, Denial Rocks

Tolle, Eckhart. *Stillness Speaks*. London: Hodder & Stoughton, 2003.

U-Haul is a trademark of U-Haul International, Inc.

Chapter 3, U-Hauls and the In-Between Place

AAA is a trademark of American Automobile Association, Inc.

"A Quote by James Baldwin." Goodreads. Goodreads. Accessed May 5, 2022.   https://www.goodreads.com/quotes/496731-any-real-change-implies-the-breakup-of-the-world-as.

Barnes & Noble is a trademark of Barnes & Noble Booksellers, Inc.

Coleman is a trademark of Coleman Company, Inc.

IHOP is a trademark of IHOP Restaurants LLC.

Martin, Civilla Durfee, and Gabriel, Charles Hutchinson. "His Eye is On the Sparrow." 1905.

M&M's is a trademark of Mars, Incorporated.

Peloton is a trademark of Peloton Interactive, Inc.

The Flinstones are a trademark of Screen Gems, Inc.

U-Haul is a trademark of U-Haul International, Inc.

Chapter 4, Make a Humble Entrance

"300 Ultimate Motivational Quotes for Personal Growth: Sharp Quotes." Sharp Quotes | Motivational Quotes | Inspirational Quotes, May 17, 2021. https://sharpquotes.com/300-ultimate-motivational-quotes-for-personal-growth/.

Chapter 5, Don't Refuse the Pounding

Louis F. Post/the personality of Henry George--1930. Accessed May 5, 2022. https://www.cooperative-individualism.org/post-louis_personality-of-henry-george-1930.htm.

Chapter 6, The Disaffected Serve Roast Beef

"Picasso Quotes." Goodreads. Goodreads. Accessed May 5, 2022. https://www.goodreads.com/author/quotes/7904800.Picasso.

Chapter 7, Be Wary of the Cheek Kissers

"A Quote by Mignon McLaughlin." Goodreads. Goodreads. Accessed May 6, 2022. https://www.goodreads.com/quotes/902327-it-s-the-most-unhappy-people-who-most-fear-change.

Coppola, Francis Ford, dir. *The Godfather.* Paramount Pictures, 1972. Film.

Gladwell, Malcolm. *Blink.* New York: Back Bay Books, 2007.

Chapter 8, Find Disciples and Drive the Ford LTD

Chevy Nova is a trademark of General Motors Corporation.

Dodge Dart is a trademark of Chrysler LLC.

Ford LTD is a trademark of Ford Motor Company.

Spicer, Edward H. *Human Problems in Technological Change.* New Jersey: John Wiley & Sons, 1952.

Toyota is a trademark of Toyota Jidosha Kabushiki Kaisha.

Chapter 9, Discerning Between Pebbles and Stones

Corningware is a trademark of Corning Incorporated.

Ford LTD is a trademark of Ford Motor Company.

Friedkin, William, dir. *The Exorcist*. Warner Bros. Pictures, 1973. Film.

Heber, Reginald. "Holy, Holy, Holy! Lord God Almighty!" 1826.

"Marianne Williamson Quote." Quotefancy. Accessed May 6, 2022. https://quotefancy.com/quote/860488/Marianne-Williamson-Birth-is-violent-whether-it-be-the-birth-of-a-child-or-the-birth-of.

Redskins is a trademark of Pro-Football, Inc.

Stites, Edgar Page. "Beluah Land." 1876.

Watts, Isaac, and Wilby, Philip. "When I Survey the Wondrous Cross." 1707.

Chapter 10, Action and the Altar Call

"A Quote by Marilyn Ferguson." Goodreads. Goodreads. Accessed May 6, 2022. https://www.goodreads.com/quotes/24386-it-s-not-so-much-that-we-re-afraid-of-change-or.

Elliott, Charlotte. "Just As I Am." 1835.

Chapter 11, Positive Energy - Avoiding the Prayer Bench

Herodotus. "Diseases always attack men when they are exposed to change." n.d.

Chapter 12, When it's Time to Preach that Sermon

Conner, Daryl. *Managing at the Speed of Change: How Resilient Managers Succeed and Prosper Where Others Fail*. New York: Random House, 2006.

"The Complete Essays of Mark Twain Quotes by Mark Twain." Goodreads. Goodreads. Accessed May 11, 2022. https://www. goodreads.com/work/quotes/38480-the-complete-essays-of-mark-twain.

Chapter 13, Make the Change Mission Live

Wheatley, Margaret. *Leadership and the New Science: Discovering Order in a Chaotic World.* 2nd ed. San Francisco: Berrett-Koehler, 1999.

Chapter 14, When the Worst Singers Want Solos

"10 Best Quotes to Direct Your Life." Articleslash.net. Accessed May 11, 2022. https://www.articleslash.net/Self-Improvement/Success/ 446830__10-Best-Quotes-To-Direct-Your-Life.html.

Chicago Bears are a trademark of Chicago Bears Football Club, Inc.

Green Bay Packers are a trademark of Green Bay Packers, Inc.

Kristofferson, Kristoffer. "Why Me." Monument Records, 1973.

Tupperware is a trademark of Dart Industries Inc.

Chapter 15, When Retired People Kill Your Dishwasher

"Louise Colet Quote." Quotefancy. Accessed May 11, 2022. https:// quotefancy.com/quote/1703157/Louise-Colet-Alas-How-enthusiasm-decreases-as-our-experience-increases

Chapter 16, Driving a Taxi that says "Jesus Saves"

"A Quote by George Eliot." Goodreads. Goodreads. Accessed May 11, 2022. https://www.goodreads.com/quotes/40245-our-deeds-determine-us-as-much-as-we-determine-our.

Wolf, Dick. Whole. *Law & Order*. NBC, 1990.

Chapter 17, Nervous Laughter and False Teeth

"A Quote by Sir Winston Churchill." Goodreads. Goodreads. Accessed May 11, 2022. https://www.goodreads.com/quotes/857718-we-make-a-living-by-what-we-get-but-we.

E. O. Excell, E. O., and Newton, John. "Amazing Grace." 1779.

Chapter 18, Mrs. Robinson and Wasps

"A Quote by Agnes Repplier. Goodreads. Goodreads. Accessed May 11, 2022. https://www.goodreads.com/quotes/84113-we-cannot-really-love-anybody-with-whom-we-never-laugh.

"A Quote by Milton Berle." Goodreads. Goodreads. Accessed May 11, 2022. https://www.goodreads.com/quotes/66479-laughter-is-an-instant-vacation.

Simon & Garfunkel. "Mrs. Robinson." Columbia, 1968.

Chapter 19, Squeezing Tithe Out of a Turnip

"A Quote by Anne Morrow Lindbergh." Goodreads. Goodreads. Accessed May 11, 2022. https://www.goodreads.com/quotes/16670-good-communication-is-as-stimulating-as-black-coffee-and-just.

Chapter 20, Betty and Her Bible

"A Quote by Anne Frank." Goodreads. Goodreads. Accessed May 11, 2022. https://www.goodreads.com/quotes/189004-how-lovely-to-think-that-no-one-need-wait-a.

"Faye Wattleton Quotes." BrainyQuote. Xplore. Accessed May 12, 2022. https://www.brainyquote.com/quotes/faye_wattleton_131845.

SAT is a trademark of College Entrance Examination Board.

Chapter 21, Baptisms, New Beginnings, and Tidal Waves

NFL is a trademark of National Football League.

YMCA is a trademark of National Council of Young Men's Christian Associations of the United States of America.

Chapter 22, Sunrise Breakthroughs

"A Quote by Jean Giraudoux." Goodreads. Goodreads. Accessed May 12, 2022. https://www.goodreads.com/quotes/357947-sadness-flies-on-the-wings-of-the-morning-and-out.

Lowry, Robert. "Low in the Grave He Lay." 1874.

Whoville is a trademark of Dr. Seuss Enterprises, L.P.

Chapter 23, Blest Be the Tie

Fawcett, John. "Blest Be the Tie That Binds." 1782.

"Quotes - Thomas Brown (the United Kingdom)." Goodreads. Goodreads. Accessed May 12, 2022. https://www.goodreads.com/quotes/list/28387446-thomas-brown.

U-Haul is a trademark of U-Haul International, Inc.

Chapter 24, The Future of Change

7-Eleven is a trademark of 7-Eleven, Inc.

"A Quote by Tuli Kupferberg." Goodreads. Goodreads. Accessed May 12, 2022. https://www.goodreads.com/quotes/57149-when-patterns-are-broken-new-worlds-emerge.

Fanta is a trademark of The Coca Cola Company.

Hope Diamond is a trademark of Smithsonian Institution.

Hornet is a trademark of FCA US LLC.

Rodgers, Richard. "Edelweiss." *The Sound of Music*. 20th Century Fox, 1965.

Stuckey's is a trademark of Stuckey's Corporation.

Willis, Wallace. "Swing Low Sweet Chariot." Circa 1865.

Chapter 25, Final Change Lessons

"Spirituality & Practice." Spiritual Quotation by Charles Dubois. Accessed May 12, 2022. https://www.spiritualityandpractice.com/quotes/quotations/view/36587/spiritual-quotation.

www.ingramcontent.com/pod-product-compliance
Lightning Source LLC
Chambersburg PA
CBHW071223210326
41597CB00016B/1927